D1204621

BuckyWorks

Anne Fuller drew this portrait of her husband at work in 1928. He's probably working on Lightful Housing.

AF October /28

Fig. 0-1

BuckyWorks

BUCKMINSTER FULLER'S IDEAS FOR TODAY

J. Baldwin

WILEY

Book Design and Production

Kathleen O'Neill and Winslow Colwell

This publication is designed to provide accurate and
authoritative information in regard to the subject
matter covered. It is sold with the understanding that
the publisher is not engaged in rendering legal, accounting,
or other professional services. If legal advice or other
expert assistance is required, the services of a competent
professional person should be sought.

Library of Congress Cataloging-in Publication Data:

Baldwin, J. 1933-
    BuckyWorks : Buckminster Fuller's ideas for today / J. Baldwin
        p.   cm.
    Includes bibliographical references and index.
    ISBN 0-471-12953-4 (alk. paper)
    ISBN 0-471-19812-9 (paper)
    1. Fuller, R. Buckminster (Richard Buckminster), 1895-1983
2. Engineers—United States—Biography. 3, Architects—United
States—Biography. 4. Inventors—United States—Biography.
I. Title.
TA140.F9B35 1996
620' . 0092—dc20   95-26003

Printed in the United States of America

20 19 18 17 16 15 14 13 12 11

Dedication

To make the world work
In the shortest possible time
Through spontaneous cooperation
Without ecological offense
Or the disadvantage of anyone.
—*R. Buckminster Fuller*

This book is dedicated to
everyone working toward this goal.

(Incidentally, Bucky denied
that this goal is altruistic. To him,
it was just good sense.)—JB

Acknowledgments

Special thanks to Bonnie Goldstein DeVarco, who knows where the treasure lies buried in the largely unexplored 45 tons of archives at the Buckminster Fuller Institute in Santa Barbara, CA. No Bonnie, no book; it's as simple as that. And she did it all in addition to her usual duties, not to mention nursing young Nicholas, who emitted no unseemly shrieks for three weeks. Institute Director Tony DeVarco, with colleagues John Ferry and Jackie Lohrke, made my life a lot easier (Jackie managed to talk someone into letting me camp in the parking lot for three weeks.) Allegra Fuller Snyder encouraged me to do the deed and cleared the way. Closer to home, Jerry George found me a publisher; my patient wife, Liz Fial, fed the starving keyboarder; and my Wiley editor, Amanda Miller, cracked a velvet whip while her assistant, MaryAlice Yates, made sure my needs were met. Maroon Tabbal labored long and hard on the geometry drawings and their explanations; Winslow Colwell, Robert Cumberford, Liz Fial, and Malcolm Wells produced illustrations on short notice. Robert Gray and Kirby Urner made sure I saw things I needed to know about. Christian Overland, Bill Perk, Charles Peck ("Wink"), Medard Gabel, and Chris Zelov gave good advice and helped stir the pot. E. J. Applewhite, Bucky's friend and collaborator, kept me honest. Dorothy Dunn, Education Director at the Cooper-Hewitt National Design Museum in New York, provided me a venue for trying out some of my ideas. Peter Meisen at GENI got a bunch of us Bucky folks together for a 100th birthday celebration. And my friends at *Whole Earth Review* kindly refrained from hassling me about missing their deadlines. —JB

Credits and Copyrights

Buckminster Fuller repeated his major concepts, themes, anecdotes, and examples—with minor differences (and occasional inconsistencies)—throughout his lectures and writings. This book is an introduction, not an academic treatise. I have made no attempt to footnote paraphrases, quotes and concepts, but I have taken care to identify what is certainly his. I accept responsibility for any errors in my story. They are inadvertent.

Most of the photographs in this book are copyrighted by the Buckminster Fuller Institute, or Allegra Fuller Snyder (as indicated below), and are used courtesy of the Buckminster Fuller Institute in Santa Barbara, California. Photographers are identified where possible, but many photographs in the Fuller Archive are unmarked and unattributed. When action was afoot, Bucky was usually armed with a camera or two. Some of the uncredited shots are doubtless by him, but there is no way to be sure.

Direct quotes and excerpts from books by Buckminster Fuller are used by permission. The words Dymaxion, Spaceship Earth, and the design of the Fuller Projection map are registered trademarks of the Buckminster Fuller Institute.

The account, *Learning a Lot, Learning Fast* (Page 142), is used with the kind permission of Amy C. Edmondson.

Credits for photographs and drawings. (All others are unknown.)

Fig. 0-1 — Anne Hewlett Fuller

Fig. 0-2 — Phil Haggerty

Fig. 1-1 — Robert Snyder

Fig. 2-1 — R. Buckminster Fuller

Fig. 2-5 — F. S. Lincoln

Figs. 2-6, 2-7 — Malcolm Wells

Fig. 2-14 — Ernest Weissman

Figs. 2-12, 2-16 — Butler Manufacturing Company

Fig. 2-17 — J. Baldwin

Figs. 2-18, 2-19 — Michael Jantzen

Figs. 2-39, 2-40, 2-41 — J. Baldwin

Figs. 3-2, 3-3, 3-4, 3-5, 3-6, 3-7, 3-8, 3-9 — Maroon Tabbal

Figs. 3-7, 3-8 — Liz Fial

Fig. 3-10 — Laura Wulf, courtesy Donald Ingber, M. D.

Fig. 4-17 — Kaufmann & Fabry

Fig. 4-22 — Robert Cumberford

Fig. 4-23 — Reprinted from Think, © 1968 by International Business Machines, Inc.

Fig. 4-24 — John Loëngard

Figs. 4-25, 4-26 — Platt Monfort

Fig. 5-1 — Charles Eames

Fig. 5-4 — Winslow Colwell

Figs. 6-4, 6-5, 6-6 — Ralph Mills

Figs. 6-9, 6-10, 6-ll, 6-12 — Kenneth Oberg

Fig. 7-4 — Official U.S. Marine Corps Photograph

Fig. 7-10 — Courtesy of The North Face

Fig. 7-11 — Alec Harrison

Fig. 8-5 — A. R. Sinsabaugh

Figs. 8-8, 8-10 — drawings by John Rauma

Figs. 8-11, 8-12 — Martin Growald

Fig. 8-14 — Don Richter

Fig. 8-21 — Jean-François Cloutier, La Biosphére

Figs. 8-22, 8-23, 8-24, 8-25 — J. Baldwin

Figs. 8-26, 8-27, 8-28, 8-29, 8-30 — © 1982 by Robert Sardinski

Fig. 8-30 — © 1981 by John Katzenberger

Fig. 8-32 — © 1979 by John and Nancy Jack Todd. Drawing by Paul Sun. Design by John Todd, Malcolm Wells, and J. Baldwin.

Figs. 10-2, 10-3 — © 1994 by the World Game Institute

Fig. 10-4 — © Global Energy Network, International (GENI). Dymaxion Map courtesy of The Buckminster Fuller Institute

Fig. 10-5 — Roger Stoller

Figs. 10-6, 10-7 — J. Baldwin

Fig. 10-10 — John Kuhtik

Fig. 10-11 — © Team Syntegrity, Inc. Drawings by Joe Truss

Fig. 11-1 — Charles Eames

Preface

R. Buckminster Fuller intentionally worked fifty years ahead of his time. That's now. Thirteen years after his death, his ideas, discoveries, and inventions offer solutions to many of our most severe worldwide problems. Yet many people are not familiar with him or his work.

That isn't surprising. Born in 1895, he was a child of another era, a time before automobiles, aircraft, radio, television, computers, and moonwalking. But Bucky (*everybody* called him Bucky) grew up, wide awake, right along with those inventions. Most of his contemporaries regarded the rapidly accelerating new technologies in terms of profits and military superiority—as a means of ensuring their survival as an elite "fittest." But Bucky saw that technology could be used to abolish poverty, hunger, and war by using the world's resources for the good of all.

Politics had not been able to accomplish that, and never would. Only energy-efficient, resource-efficient design could "make the world work for everyone" for the first time in history. In 1927 Bucky started what he called a "design science revolution" to bring this about. He set out to show what one ordinary person could do as a design scientist.

Totally committed, and working at a furious pace, Bucky accomplished much in the following fifty-six years. He worked hard right up to his dying day in 1983. But the design science revolution is far from over, and there is a new urgency: It is becoming clear that we are about to find out whether humans will be a success on Earth, or fail as a species. Bucky was optimistic that we *could* make it, but not that we *would*.

Everything Bucky did was intended to help us succeed. In this book, I introduce some (but not all) of the major ideas, inventions, and discoveries that he developed for our use. Instead of the gee-whiz aspects, I've focused on the logic behind his work, and how he nurtured his ideas from paper napkin scribbles to proof-of-concept demonstrations.

To me, Bucky's most important work was as a teacher, though he didn't like being seen as a guru. To spread his ideas, he wrote twenty-three books, taught hundreds of seminars, and lectured extensively. He insisted that his domes and other inventions were mainly built to demonstrate pure principle at work. He was showing us how to think.

My intent is to let his example inspire you to work on the important problems that still must be solved. Bucky certainly left us plenty to work with. —JB

A Grain of Salt

To keep things clear, I'd better present my credentials: Buckminster Fuller entered my life while I was a freshman design student at the University of Michigan in 1952. His stunning fourteen-hour lecture questioned the validity of everything I'd been taught, yet reinforced what I'd learned on my own. That inspired me to live my life as a grand experiment with myself as the guinea pig—just as he did, but following my own interests. So far, things have gone well.

Over thirty-one years, I attended many of his marathon lectures, seminars, and World Game workshops, taught for him one year at Southern Illinois University, and have had a hand in designing and building thirty-six experimental domes, including one on the Fuller family's Bear Island off the Maine coast. The hours of one-on-one time I had with him were mostly spent in limits-testing argument.

Fig. 0-2

Bucky and the author at the opening ceremony for the New Alchemy Institute's "Pillowdome" bioshelter, 1982.

By example, he encouraged me to think for myself comprehensively, to be disciplined, to work for the good of everyone, and to have a good time doing it. I can't remember looking at life any other way. The above certainly does not make me a protegé, but I may well be one of his artifacts. Please keep that in mind as you read.

Note that this is not a biography or a scholarly, footnoted critique of Bucky's work. Other authors have already done that well. I do not presume to speak for Bucky; after all, he took nearly thirteen-hundred pages to explain just one of his concepts (synergetics). My quotations and paraphrases are mostly from notes taken at his lectures and during our talks, but all of these ideas appear repeatedly in various forms throughout his writings and taped lectures. This book is intended to get you interested in finding out more. Nobody does Bucky better than Bucky. —JB

Contents

Chapter 1

The Mission of Guinea Pig B

It was jump, or think. —RBF

Success and Failure

"I'd like to introduce myself as the world's most successful failure."
R. Buckminster Fuller often launched his lectures with those startling words.
Chunky and forthright, he did not have the looks or demeanor of an unsuccessful man. By conventional standards, however, he was a failure: Harvard
had dismissed (he said "fired") him twice—the first time for taking a New York
chorus line to dinner instead of taking his midterm exams. After the first firing,
his outraged family shipped him off to learn some responsibility as an apprentice machinist in a Canadian cotton mill. He was, after all, the fifth generation
of Fullers to attend Harvard. Margaret Fuller, the famous feminist/transcendentalist, was his great aunt.

The mill gave him a dirty-hands feel for machinery and engineering that
can only be gained by making, installing and troubleshooting complex
mechanisms. (At that time, most technology was understandable by looking
at it.) He also learned firsthand about the world of the blue-collar worker—
experience that was rare among old-guard New England families. He did
so well that his family and Harvard relented.

Fig. 1-1

Bucky and Anne Fuller. Their daughter, Allegra Fuller Snyder, says this
photograph clearly reveals the spirit of a marriage that lasted 66 years.

Unfortunately, his good performance in the cotton mill did not signal an improved respect for academia. Expelled a second time for "showing insufficient interest in his studies," he got a job wrestling sides of beef in a meat-packing house. Bucky (everyone but his wife called him Bucky), never did acquire a college degree or the requisite awe of academe.

A stint as a Naval officer in World War I put his experience to work. He had the good luck to be assigned to a ship involved with wireless communications and aircraft—the most advanced technology of that era. Mechanical skills and ingenuity honed at the mill gave him the know-how to recognize and solve the problem of extracting pilots from ditched aircraft before they drowned. He designed a boom that enabled the crash boat to yank the aircraft from the water in seconds.

The Navy rewarded him with a few months at Annapolis, where he learned to think in terms of global communications, air travel, and logistics—all of which would become central to his future work. He had no trouble with those courses, and he recognized why: They dealt with reality—often a very harsh reality. Learning was easy for him when theory was connected to experience.

The war over, he resigned from the Navy and joined the seething pre-stock-market-crash business world of the 1920s. For a while, things went well for the aggressive, hard-drinking young Bucky. While in the Navy, he had married Anne Hewlett, the daughter of a prominent architect. They had a baby. He founded the Stockade Building System, making his father-in-law's patented fiber-concrete building blocks. Then, in 1922, disaster struck. This time, it was more serious than a student's problems with the dean. Bucky and Anne lost their first child to disease that he partially blamed on his inability to provide her with healthy living conditions.

Determined to do better, he worked furiously to win acceptance for his Stockade system. Acceptance proved to be a frustrating, and ultimately unachievable goal. He sold about 240 buildings, but the business was being strangled by local codes that required him to seek approval for each structure. Then, at the height of the struggle, a takeover drove him out of his own company, ruining him financially, and losing his friends' money as well.

That blow brought him to a standstill. He was a failure, a "throwaway," as he said. He had a healthy new daughter, but no job. He would not be able to take proper care of her, either. Worse, he had little incentive to get a new job and work hard in the same corrupt system that had put him out on the street through no fault of his own. It was the low point of his life. He considered suicide. "It was jump or think," he said. He chose think.

I saw that there was nothing to stop me from trying to think about our total planet Earth and thinking realistically about how to operate it on an enduringly sustainable basis as the magnificent human-passengered spaceship that it is. —RBF

The crisis caused Bucky to consider carefully what people were for. He reasoned that humans, including himself, must have been made for some purpose. He determined to find out what that was—perhaps he'd been doing the wrong thing. (He did not consider that life might be meaningless, perhaps because his Fuller forefathers included many clergymen.)

Bucky noticed that Universe seemed to take care of all living things as long as they instinctively performed their designed roles ("Fish don't have to pay for swimming in the sea"). Humans must have been designed to be a success. We've been here for millions of years. We must have a role to play in Universe. Thomas Malthus was wrong. (In 1810, Malthus had determined that population was outstripping supply, ensuring the permanent us-or-them condition that underlies politics and strife.) That was a brave conclusion, considering that the great majority of humans at that time lived short lives in desperate poverty.

At his birth in 1895, Bucky's own life expectancy in a rapidly developing industrial society was just 42 years. His elders had advised him that to live even that long would require him to take advantage of other humans. For him to live well, others would have to suffer—a well-proved recipe for incessant war. Someone had just taken advantage of him, and he didn't like it. People should not have to live like beasts.

He reasoned that humans differ from other animals in only one important way; we have minds. We can think. We are designed and built to think, and then act on those thoughts. We are the only animal that can control (to a degree) our own evolution—toward success or toward failure. We have been designed to do this. Other animals are much more automated than humans. If we behave like mindless animals, we may survive briefly, but our species will fail in the long run. If we use our minds for making humanity a success on Earth, Universe will take care of us, too.

Bucky concluded that he had no right to commit suicide—his unique experience might make a critical difference to the fate of humanity. He decided to "commit egocide" instead.

Bucky joins construction workers after hours for a salutary swing around the Dome Restaurant in Woods Hole, MA (see also Fig. 5-2). He had a good sense of humor, and was inclined to be downright playful when work was going well. Despite his hard-driving schedule, Bucky did, in fact, "stop to smell the flowers."

Fig. 1-2

Then, he got to work. His goal was "… a lifelong experiment designed to discover what—if anything—a healthy young male human of average size, experience, and capability with an economically dependent wife and newborn child, starting without capital or any kind of wealth, cash savings, account monies, credit, or university degree, could effectively do that could not be done by great nations or great private enterprise to lastingly improve the physical protection and support of all human lives, at the same time removing undesirable restraints and improving individual initiatives of any and all humans aboard our planet Earth." A big order, one that could only be filled by a lifetime experiment. He appointed himself Guinea Pig B (for Bucky) to carry it out.

But where to start? Unlike most hotheads, Bucky had no respect for politics. The re-formed Bucky only trusted experience. Experience showed him that politics was based on fear and ignorance (he said *ignore*-ance), was structurally dishonest, and was ineffective in the long run. Politics always tries to pull down those at the top instead of pulling up those on the bottom. "Politics always ends up with the guns," he said. Mere reform wouldn't work. A new form might.

His alternative to politics was radical and deeply subversive. If we are designed like other animals to be a success, then nature must have provided enough of everything needed for all to live a healthy existence. People living well would have little interest in fighting and destruction. Bucky decided that reliable information and efficient design could identify and fairly distribute the Earth's resources, bringing a good life to all. Developing that information and putting it to work would be the mission of Guinea Pig B.

The Chronofile

According to the truckers who moved it in 1994, Bucky's archive weighs about 45 tons!

Bucky had been keeping scrapbooks of things that interested him since 1907, but he didn't officially name his collection "Chronofile" until a decade later. His realized that a career as a guinea pig would need to be recorded as a means of integrating his self-image with how others regarded him, and as credible proof of what one person could do to make the world work. Experimenters should always keep records for scientific credibility.

The Chronofile had already revealed that he did best when he was working on behalf of others rather than for himself. The more people that would benefit from his work, the better he did. He had done well in the Navy where he could innovate without having to show a profit. The Chronofile proved that doing what needed to be done wasn't being "recklessly altruistic"; it was being ultimately practical.

Bucky studied the Chronofile as a means of detecting macro-trends that were otherwise difficult to see in gee-whiz-driven public media. For instance, the Chronofile not only recorded the many new inventions and technologies that were appearing in the early 1900s, it clearly showed that the *rate* of innovation and social change was increasing rapidly. This gave Bucky the numbers he needed to make his gestation curves. Continuing the curves led him to call some of his predictions "inevitabilities." He wasn't always right about when a change would occur. Things often happened somewhat later than he said (or hoped?) they would, but he was quite accurate in what the result would be (Fig. 10-1).

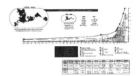

Over the years, the Chronofile received sketches, clippings, statistics, trends, interesting new technologies, all of his correspondence (including love letters with carbon copies of his answers), even traffic tickets and dry cleaning bills. Certain occurrences that might be painful or embarrassing to others (and possibly to himself) were not recorded—the time he overturned his own Dymaxion car, for instance.

Some of the items he did keep are deeply personal evidence of the price he paid for his way of life: In the Chronofile for 1933, there is a letter from his young daughter asking when she was going to see him again. Work on the Dymaxion car kept him from home for months at a time. Obviously, he would not have kept such material if he had not intended that people read it someday. He wanted readers to understand how and why he hurtled through life as he did. He intent was not to brag, but to instruct and inspire.

The Chronofile is augmented by quantities of drawings, models, video and audio tapes, 64,000 feet of movie film, 50,000 slides and photographs, and 35 file drawers of manuscripts (including several unpublished books). He also kept a clipping file and a library of books that had influenced his thinking. The complete trove probably makes Bucky the most thoroughly documented 20th-century man. He intended that the Chronofile should be used to fashion a definitive biography that would be an inspiring example of what one person could do. That biography has yet to be written.

Wind Sucks

I made up my mind as a Rule of Communication that I wouldn't care if I was not understood—so long as I was not misunderstood. —RBF

Bucky tells of spending his post-crisis year (1928) in wordless silence while exorcising thoughtlessly held beliefs not based on experience or science. "It was a little hard on my wife," he quipped, but the Chronofile shows that he gave lectures during that time. Bucky often spoke in metaphor, and was not above an occasional parable. It was during that time that he developed his accurate, but sometimes opaque, language for expressing his ideas.

At his best, Bucky illuminated his insights in a way that changed your thought patterns, and spurred introspection. At other times, despite (or because of) his desire to be absolutely clear, even the cleverest translators are of limited help to his readers and listeners. The density of information is daunting. A single sentence might contain the seeds of an entirely new vision of physics.

He challenged your own word use as well. When Bucky announced that wind "sucked," his audience usually laughed out loud. The statement certainly sounded funny, but he was serious. Talking about the wind "blowing" deflects the thoughts of speaker and listeners alike from what is actually happening. No force can push a huge parcel of air around Earth any more than you can push a flock of ducks into a barn. Push—compression—is local. Push doesn't operate over long distances. In any case, what could be doing the pushing?

Nothing is doing the pushing; wind isn't pushed. When you face the wind, you have your back to its cause. A distant low pressure area pulls denser air to itself, just as a bucket of feed in the barn will bring in the ducks. Suck—tension—can operate over vast distances. Suction is not deterred by obstacles. A northwest wind is actually a southeast suck. Our parents and teachers have told us wrong. As a consequence, we think about wind—and doubtless other related phenomena—in unrealistic and inappropriate ways. Bucky wanted us to question everything we have been told. If our teachers couldn't get wind right, how can we trust anything else they say?

Bucky was also annoyed by "sunrise" and "sunset." It frustrated him that even astronomers mindlessly used terms inherited from a time when people thought the earth was flat. He felt so strongly about this that he offered a prize to anyone who could come up with a better way of saying sunrise and sunset. (Nobody won.)

Bucky also insisted, "If you still use the terms up and down, you're still thinking in terms from the dark ages." There is no "up" or "down," only "in" or "out." In is specific—in toward the center of the earth. No more upside-down Chinese dangling by their feet. *Out* is going anywhere away from the center of the earth. Except in a very local way—a carpenter's plumb-bob, for instance—up and down are deceptive, flat-earth terms. But on a structure the length of the Verazzano suspension bridge connecting Staten Island to Brooklyn, the two plumb-bob-vertical towers are spaced so widely on Earth's curved surface that they "lean" away from one another. Their tops are 1.62 inches (4.1 cm) further apart than their footings! That's the reality that "up" and "down" don't describe.

Is all this just semantic niggling? Not to Bucky. To him it was both pragmatic and a matter of principle. Language is a tool. Accurate word use sharpens communication. He wanted us to think about what we were saying. How could students gain a proper feel for Universe if they were taught common terms and phrases that wrongly described what was really going on?

His own talk was disciplined. He never used cuss words. He could be adamant about other people's chatter. On one occasion during an eclipse of the moon, a relative remarked excitedly that the shadow was "coming across the moon more from the top than the side." Bucky, usually polite, growled, "The moon doesn't *have* any *top*, stupid," causing a wave of muffled snickers. He sometimes berated associates and students for making puns—language is already imprecise without your making it worse. But he did that with a wicked glitter in his eye; he was notorious for his own bad puns.

Bucky was aware that manipulating popular word usage is difficult, but he knew (from experience, of course) that it could be done. He coined and used the word 'debunk' in 1927, then noted with satisfaction how fast it spread. The Chronofile has newspaper clipping proof.

Chapter 2

The Lightful House

You can't better the world by simply talking to it.
Philosophy to be effective must be mechanically applied. —RBF

Life in 4D

Guinea Pig B put his reconstituted language to use in 1928 with a self-published potboiler of a book, *4D Timelock,* in which he proposed a new sort of shelter. (The "4D" label carried a whiff of fourth-dimension; Einstein's work was just becoming accessible to nonscientists.) Bucky focused on shelter because small building design and construction technology was the only major human endeavor that had not yet joined the industrial revolution. The technology of a typical house was very nearly the same as its counterpart in the 18th century, and was thoroughly obsolete. All buildings but skyscrapers depended on gravity and friction for their strength, just as buildings had for thousands of years. Even brilliantly engineered skyscrapers used much of their steel inefficiently in compression.

Putting aside all thought of quick profits, Bucky decided to design buildings that he probably wouldn't live long enough to see. He expected a half-century wait because his Chronofile showed that various technologies have a gestation period—the time between their conception and their introduction into the marketplace. The gestation period is in direct proportion to the speeds involved in the technology under study. Electronics move at about the speed of light.

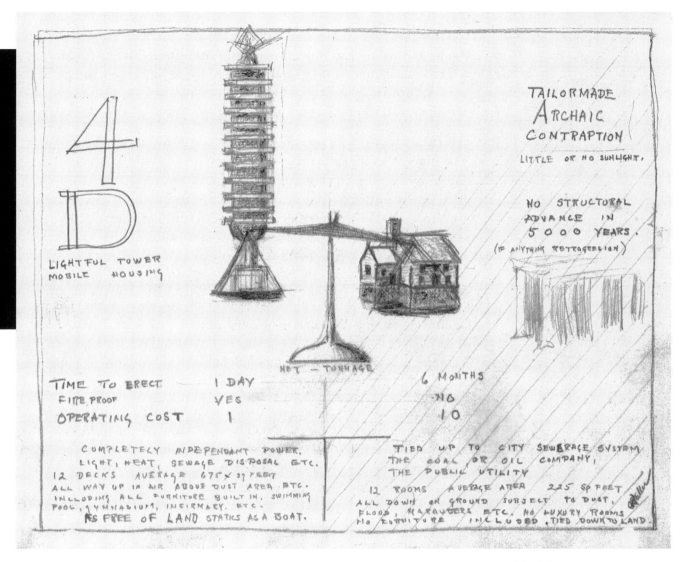

Fig. 2-1

Breakthroughs in electronics take a bit less than two years. The most advanced aircraft, at Mach 3, take ten years. Major changes in autos appear in fifteen to twenty-five years, partly because there is little incentive to truly advance until forced to by regulations.

Buildings generally don't move at all until torn down. New designs and construction techniques gestate slowly, taking a generation or more to achieve acceptance. Much of that delay can be traced to owners and lenders, who do not wish to see their equity and collateral outmoded.

Advances in architecture are also stymied by building codes. There are two kinds: specification and performance. Specification codes name materials and the conditions for their application. "Interior walls shall be framed in construction grade fir 2x4 lumber, spaced vertically 16 inches on center" doesn't leave much room for innovations, as Bucky found out with his Stockade System blocks.

Performance codes give more opportunity, but it comes at a price. A performance code might set strength, fire resistance, and soundproofing standards, but will not say how the requirements are to be met. Performance codes are rare. They require extra thought by designers, extra care by builders, and extra work by inspectors. They invite controversy and lawsuits. Defiance of codes is unwise. Ultimately, all codes are enforced by armed police, even in a democracy. No wonder so few new ideas are seen in building!

Bucky assumed—rather naively—that public enthusiasm for a logical new idea would surely vanquish the institutional barriers to its acceptance. Rather than safely modifying existing structures to be more efficient and easier to make—a modernized Cape Cod bungalow, for instance—he started fresh with a radical design that included many of the features he would use in his future dwelling designs. He dubbed his proposed structure the "Lightful House."

The design had no basis whatever in traditional architectural styles; why should a house resemble a Greek temple or an Italian villa? Bucky had no interest in fads and arty expression. Despite the fact that his father-in-law was a famous architect, he publicly dismissed all architects as "exterior decorators." In return, most architects dismissed his ideas as unaesthetic industrial products, like locomotives. Frank Lloyd Wright was one of the few who understood what Bucky was trying to do. He and a handful of others were also experimenting with industrialized housing. Their work can be seen in the fascinating book, *Yesterday's Houses of Tomorrow*, by H. Jandl, J. Burns, and M. Auer (1991, Preservation Press). It shows clearly that no other design went nearly as far as Bucky's Lightful House.

Ephemeralization

Bucky's design process started with a long list of performance criteria that any house should meet. Among them were mass-producibility, strength, low maintenance, and light weight (for deliverability by zeppelin)—all attributes of aluminum. Aluminum was expensive, however, so materials efficiency was the only logical move.

Bucky shows his first attempt at a tension structure. Think of the hexagonal rings as big, lumpy bicycle wheel rims on their sides. The cabling acts as spokes, and the mast as the hub. The rim and mast handle all the compression loads. Obviously, the flexible cables can only carry tension. It is a light, strong way to build. This efficient division of duty shows in all of Bucky's later structures, including his tensegrity geodesics.

Fig. 2-2

There are three basic ways to cut materials use: First, make the design smaller; second, use materials in their most efficient form (do more with less); third, use minimum-surface (hence, minimum materials) geometry. In today's lingo, we'd call it "replacing material with information." Bucky called the resulting dematerialization, "ephemeralization". When a student jokingly asked if the ultimate more-with-less was to do everything-with-nothing, Bucky said yes: Design is at its best the closer it approaches the purely metaphysical (Fig. 2-1). Ephemeralization is not something you add to a design, it occurs naturally as the result of applied natural principles. It's more of an attitude than a strategy.

Making the house smaller didn't appeal to him (though it would later). At the time, the American way of doing things tended towards bigger-is-better. In any case, his design would work in any reasonable size. He'd start with proportions that would impress sceptics and appeal to prospective (well-to-do) buyers.

Bucky knew that people with modest incomes tend to accept and follow the example of the upper class.

Efficient geometry was easy: Make the house round to minimize roof and wall area per unit of floor area, and stack the rooms to minimize land costs. Bucky took particular delight in mentioning that geometric principles were pure metaphysics: weightless and free. Nature always does things in the most economical way. By using ideal surface-to-volume ratios, 4D designs were surely more "natural" than conventional houses.

The desire to use durable construction materials in their most efficient form led him to employ metal in tension. From his childhood experience with sailboats, and his Navy experience with aircraft, Bucky had come to appreciate the use of tension. Steel, for instance, is at its most efficient when used as cable. That is why the longest bridges are suspended from a few towers. At any given moment, a bicycle is actually hanging from a few of its topmost, skinny spokes. Of course, there have to be compression members as well, but they can be minimized and optimized by separating them from tensile duties.

Bucky's first crude (not very taut) model (Fig 2-2) reveals the basic design that he would use until the discovery of geodesics. (In geodesics, he would completely separate tension members from compression members, balancing them as *tensegrity* structures (see Chapter 3). The mast and floor perimeters take the compression loads. Nearly everything else is in tension. Wall and roof materials are stretched tight. The floors are stretched netting, with pneumatic, sound-deadening coverings. "If you drop the baby, it will just bounce back". Beds and furniture are inflated. (Pneumatics are also tensile; under powerful magnification, balloons and tires can be seen as stretched geodesic nets with apertures small enough to restrain the air molecules.)

Ephemeralization also applied to energy use. Bucky regarded his 4D houses as "valves" that controlled the flow of energy, material, and light flowing between the indoors and outdoors while supporting the daily lives of the people involved. Thinking of a house as a valve leads to new ways of providing shelter. Bucky said, "Homes should be thought of as service equipment, not as monuments." This concept doesn't sound very inviting, but neither would your car or your clothes if it they were described in such terms. We have been subtly trained to think of homes in a way that no longer matches the way we actually live or want to live.

Drawn in a style that was popular in the late 1920s, this dramatic street of 10-deck 4D luxury homes has much the same "city of tomorrow" visual impact as the work of Bucky's contemporaries. But only his 10-deck houses were truly new. They expressed a separation of tension and compression made possible by invisible metallurgy. Their appearance was almost entirely a result of the principles involved, not arbitrary styling. The apparatus on the roof is a Flettner-type wind turbine driving an electric generator. Bucky insisted that air currents induced by buildings could be harnessed for power.

Fig. 2-3

4D Towers

The 4D towers (Figs.2-3, 2-4) were intended as deluxe apartments with each floor dedicated to a specific function. By stacking floors around an elevator, much less property is needed. A single entrance enhances security. The main living quarters are near the top, where air is cleaner and the view is more interesting. Ten stories puts the electricity-generating wind turbine up where the wind is, without the expense of a separate tower. At the bottom, the base

More 10-decker drama. Because the towers deployed their materials in the same way as suspension bridges, utilizing them as bridge components seemed natural. Bucky had exciting drawings made to help the public visualize the potential of his structures, but he didn't let drama degenerate into magical effects that hid the physical principles involved. Most other architects, including form-follows-function modernists, hid the real supporting structure.

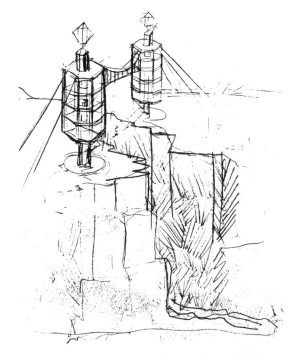

Fig. 2-4

Wind tunnel experiments with this model showed that a building's heat loss is proportional to its air drag. The streamlined fairing reduced or eliminated the need for insulation on this 4D 10-decker, and dramatically cut structural wind loads. Starling Burgess, engineer of the Dymaxion car, also engineered this. Fifteen years later, Bucky used what was learned from this experiment in the Wichita House (p. 40).

is stabilized by a swimming pool in a rather geodesic-looking reinforced container. The 10-deck towers worked out to be light enough to carry beneath the largest zeppelin, but there was no way to make them in 1928.

The 4D Dymaxion House

The towers evolved into a lower, simpler, more house-like hexagonal arrangement that was developed to highlight a (long-forgotten) furniture display for the Marshall Field department store in Chicago. The store named it the 4D "Dymaxion" House. (Fig. 2-8). Bucky's patent shows a particularly hideous square version. His attorney was afraid that a hexagonal or round building would be too unfamiliar to be credible. The Dymaxion was not the only aluminum building patented at that time, but it was the only one that used the metal to its full potential.

From the beginning, 4D Dymaxion Houses were intended to take advantage of the economies of mass production. Bucky hammered hard on the stupidity of handmaking houses that gained absolutely nothing from the handwork. In fact,

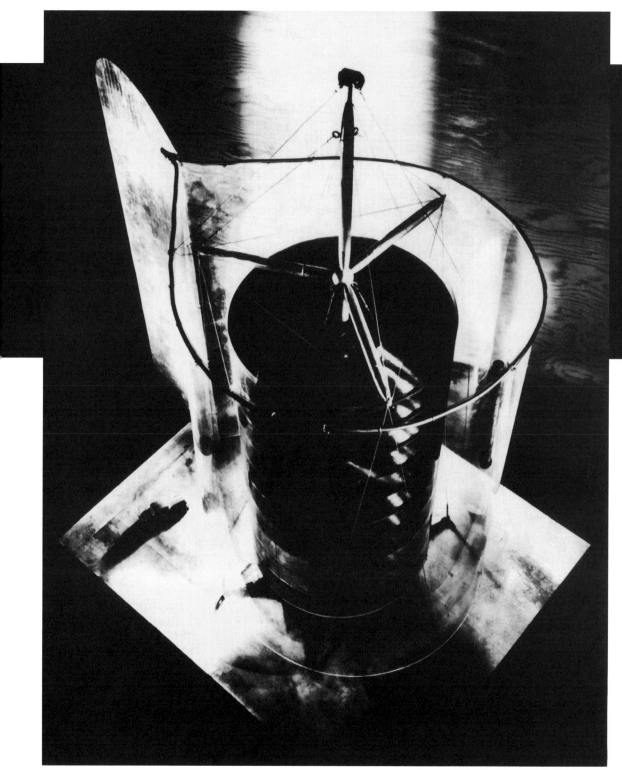

Fig. 2-5

Fig. 2-6

handicraft gave opportunity for low quality arising from careless construction. Handcrafting also requires the use of wood and other easily degraded "natural" materials. Those materials have been regarded as standard for so long that they are available only in a form that is impractical for use in nonrectangular buildings.

Bucky was fond of asking people to imagine what it would be like to order an automobile in the same way they order a house. Choose from a selection of local car designers, or acquire a catalog of standard designs. Choose from a limited selection of inappropriate styles from past centuries (Roman chariot, Louis 14th royal coach). Procure the necessary permits from the town council. Permits are awarded on a case-by-case basis.

After months of design and preparing drawings, the approvals would be signed by persons with no knowledge of automobile engineering. The bank loan officer could withhold approval until certain design changes were made to meet his or her taste. Finally, construction would begin—on your lot (Fig. 2-6).

Sheet metal workers, welders, foundrymen, upholsterers, tire makers, machinists and painters —each from a different union—would ply their trades in your driveway when weather permitted. Their materials and components would sit piled outdoors for months, vulnerable to vandals, thieves, and exposure to the elements. There would be union and supplier squabbles. An army of inspectors would harass the subcontractors at every step of the process. The job would almost certainly take longer and cost more than you had agreed.

Six months to a year after the project began, your handcrafted car would be ready for its first run. It might, or might not, perform well. It would probably cost a lot to run and maintain. The bill, in today's dollars, would come to about $300,000—the going price for a handmade car fashioned from standard parts. (A totally handmade car costs millions.) With the current usurious interest rate, you would pay almost three-quarters of a million dollars for the made-on-your-premises car. Obviously, this is not a good way to make and sell cars. To Bucky, it was obviously not a good way to make and sell houses.

Mass production had, and has, its detractors. In 1928, the American Institute of Architects (AIA) passed a resolution: "Be it resolved that the American Institute of Architects establish itself on record as inherently opposed to any peas-in-a-pod-like reproducible designs."

Bucky retorted that nature commonly makes use of repetition in cells, crystals, and eggs. Evolution tends to standardize design—you don't see animal noses in the middle of their backs. Noses are logically placed by their function.

Architect Malcolm Wells painted this impression of what a neighborhood of Dymaxion Houses might look like. Stems could be of various heights for variety, and to avoid shading solar collectors or blocking views. The sheltered space under the house could be used as a carport or for storage, with or without fence walls hung on the stabilizing cables.

Fig. 2-7

People accept and employ standardized designs, too: They have no objection to cars or books being essentially the same, for instance, and advertising often brags about a product being the "best seller". Why should houses be any different? And what most people call individuality in houses is actually just superficial decor. Their so-called individuality is actually conformity to images manipulated by others.

All Dymaxion Houses of similar design would have to be essentially identical in order to benefit from the economies and precision of mass production. The installers would not need drawings—properly designed, high-precision parts could only fit in one correct way. (Deviations from the standard design would soon lead back to handcrafting.)

Bucky's houses would express their owners' individuality by nurturing them and encouraging contemplation and innovation. The occupants would interact with a Dymaxion House in much the same way they do with a musical instrument. A piano articulates the music; a Dymaxion House articulates the desires and ideas of the people in it. It is able to change and evolve with the inhabitants. It is a place of action. Therefore, like a blank piece of drawing paper, it should be free of permanent ornament and faddish arbitrary style.

The nude model model on the model bed in this model Dymaxion House was considered a bit scandalous in 1929, as she demonstrated the precise climate control of the Dymaxion House. It was exhibited at the Marshall Field department store in Chicago. The word Dymaxion (from dynamic, maximum, and ion) was coined by an ad man who thought that 4D sounded like an apartment number. Rights to the name were assigned to Bucky as a courtesy.

Fig. 2-8

After careful analysis, Bucky discovered that a mass-produced house could be made for about the same money per-pound as a good-quality car. It would also weigh about the same—about 6000 pounds (2721 kg) in 1927. He was assuming a high-performance house made from durable materials. That meant metal—specifically aluminum.

A house made from aluminum was too much for Bucky's critics. They'd go along with the logic of a round house, but they wanted it to be fashioned from "natural" materials. Bucky pointed out that any combination of molecules that nature permits is "natural." Moreover, aluminum is the second most common element in the Earth's crust. It has a high energy cost, but it lasts indefinitely. It requires no maintenance or paint. It can be recycled. Most conventional materials have such a short life span that using them could be regarded as planned obsolescence. Old houses exist only because of incessant maintenance and occasional refurbishing.

The 4D Dymaxion House featured a main floor and an observation/garden/recreation deck. The house had a comprehensive climate control that distributed heat so evenly that bedclothes would not be necessary (Fig. 2-8). A single light source served the entire house through a system of mirrors and dimmers. The filtered ventilation system and a washer-dryer that also put the clothes away reduced housework to a minimum. Bucky asserted that nobody should "have to put in an 8-hour day devoted to yesterday's dirt."

The washer and other appliances were built into the walls and mast. When better technology appeared, the mechanical components could be easily replaced without tearing out or rebuilding anything. In that way, the house resisted the technological obsolescence that makes old houses seem old. Dymaxion appliance walls could also be used to upgrade renovated conventional houses.

It is the "go-ahead-with-life" room that represents Bucky's most advanced innovation (Fig. 2-9, library on the lower right). With a world globe, library (with O-Volving shelves), radio, television (TV had just been demonstrated then), typewriter, and drawing board, it is nothing less than a personal multimedia center—in 1927! It was a special room "where children may develop self-education on a selective basis. . . that they may go together as real individuals not crowd nonentities."

Bucky recommended a similar room for businesses. Called the "Conning Tower" after the control center on warships, it had all of the features of the home version, plus telephone, telegraph, stock ticker, audio and film facilities, mimeograph (those were the days!), and direct access to large data banks. A business owner could keep track of markets and competitors all over the world—a concept that was unheard of in the early 1930s. Except, of course, in the unheralded central control offices of the Big Players of that day.

With all those wonderful features, why didn't the 4D Dymaxion go into production? There were two reasons: First, the necessary materials were not yet available at a reasonable price. That led to the second barrier. Counting the cost of developing the necessary materials, the price tag of tooling up for production was way too high. In today's dollars it amounted to billions. As usual, it would take a war to bring out the needed money. Bucky said, "Whether this is the proper solution or not, something of its kind will be developed." He shelved the project and turned his attention to transportation. The first crude Dymaxion House did not get built until 1940, when World War II was under way.

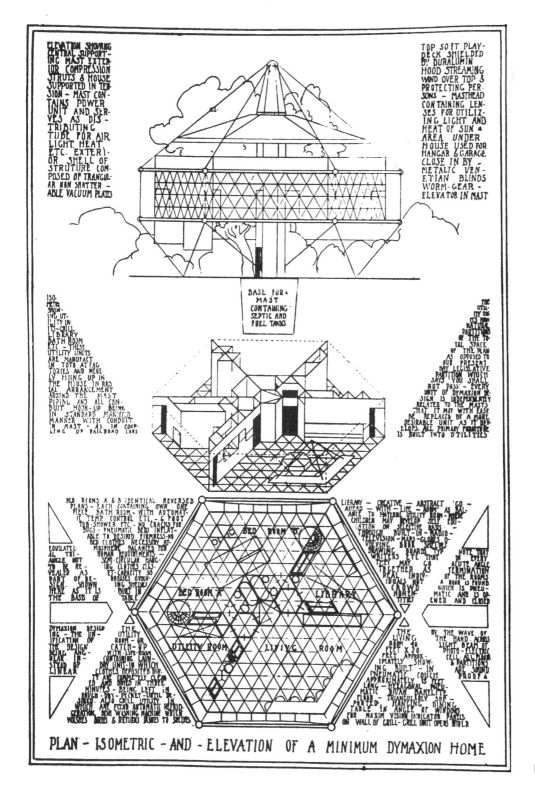

PLAN - ISOMETRIC - AND - ELEVATION OF A MINIMUM DYMAXION HOME

Fig. 2-9

Fig. 2-10

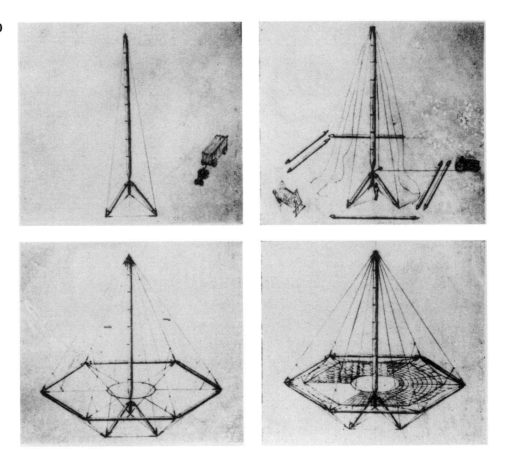

The Dymaxion Mobile Dormitory

The Dymaxion House needed a sponsor. In the United States, a tangle of building and zoning codes, bank policies, inter-union turf battles, and the Depression made progress slow. But in totalitarian Russia, a single phone call to the right person could make a project happen quickly. It was worth a try.

Bucky developed this Dymaxion housing unit for migrant farm workers, and factory workers in the many new industrial towns being built as Russia industrialized in the 1930s.

A trip to the Ural mountains gave him a taste of the difficult conditions his design would have to withstand. Field conditions (and the workers) were very rough. Manufacturing facilities were crude. Metal was scarce, and exotic materials were not available at all. (In a letter home, Bucky asked friends to send him toilet paper.) Such circumstances called for a Dymaxion design (Fig. 2-10).

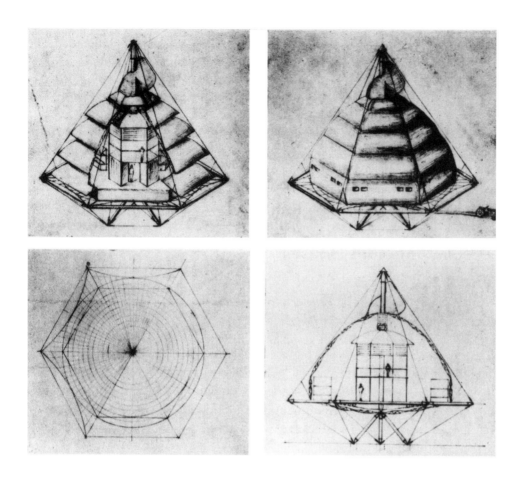

The basic scheme was the same as the original Dymaxion House, but most of the structure was made of wood and simple local materials. Floor netting was fiber rope, insulated with packed grass, and surfaced with compressed sawdust hardboard. The openable wall "petals" were hollow, fabric-covered panels much like the wings of light aircraft. Their aluminized surfaces distributed diffused sunlight from the skylight, and radiant heat and light from the white-flame kerosene/compressed air burner at the masthead. The ruddered roof-peak vent controlled air circulation when the petals were closed.

Dishes, clothes, and people were washed by water-saving "Fog Guns." A "Packaging Toilet" recovered excrement for compost or methane. (Both are discussed in more detail below.) The cooperative's tractor provided compressed air for the heat/light unit, and carried the fuel and water tanks. (Today, a tractor could be used as a "cogenerator" to furnish heat and electricity with approximately 85% efficiency.)

The low-drag shape of the Dormitory reduced the need for insulation and heavy, wind-resisting bracing, as had been demonstrated in the 4D house wind tunnel experiments. Towed to the site by the tractor, (Fig. 2-10) the building could be erected by its inhabitants (and the tractor's winch) in an hour.

The Dymaxion Mobile Dormitory was ideal technically, but not politically: Despite its utility, simplicity, and minimal use of resources, it was considered too comfortable and high-tech for a people involved in the struggle to build an egalitarian worker's society. The Soviets rejected it.

The Autonomous House

Lightful Housing, 4D, and the Dymaxion houses were all intended to be "autonomous"—able to provide a healthy living space without being hooked up to centralized utility systems. Is this desirable? Can it be done? To Bucky, autonomy was an important part of his goal of a one-town world.

If you washed the earth out from under all the buildings in a typical community, you would see that each of them is one terminal of a complex network of pipes and wires leading to and from centralized utilities and other terminals. The inevitable and absolutely necessary road net may be regarded as another part of the umbilical system that enables people, information, and goods to reach the house, and "garbage" (house exhaust) to be taken away.

It is an expensive system. Significant tax subsidy is required for its installation and maintenance. Its construction costs are a major factor in high urban land prices. The large sums involved in providing centralized services imply concentrated political power and its tempting opportunities for corruption. (Much politics has to do with whose hand is on the metaphorical faucet.) The system is also vulnerable to low bid-low quality, obsolescence, labor unrest, vandals, deferred maintenance, terrorists, and disaster.

A house gains considerable advantage from being "autonomous"—that is, from standing alone, with no need for connection to a municipal system of pipes and wires. Undeveloped land is cheaper. Utility bills are lower. Assuming quality equipment and motivated maintenance (it's yours), reliability should be better than that of complex public systems. With no large-scale hardware, and no transmission losses, overall efficiency goes up and environmental problems go down. But how is autonomy to be accomplished, and is it affordable?

It is useful to analyze any human endeavor in terms of imports and exports. A typical house imports energy (fuel, electricity, and solar), information, food, clean water, clean air, and all manner of products. It is a net consumer, but it need not be. Recent developments in superinsulation and "passive" solar design (in which the building itself collects and stores solar energy) have made furnaces and air conditioning unnecessary in all but the most extreme climates. The latest passive designs cost *less* than inefficient traditional models. Their low running costs invite better financing terms.

Photovoltaics, wind generators, and micro-hydroelectric systems can supply all electricity if the appliances and lights are chosen for efficiency. I'm writing this by the light of a compact fluorescent desk lamp that gives me as much light as a 60 watt incandescent bulb, but only draws 13 watts. An "off-the-grid" house nearby has a family-size refrigerator that demands only 10% as much power as ours. Autonomous house dwellers live well. They need only cut back on waste, and perhaps some showing-off.

In many locations, water can be collected and purified on-site. Low-wattage well pumps and water-efficient appliances are available. In most climates, the sun and waste heat can provide enough hot water for a family, though the timing of showers and clothes washing may have to be adjusted to solar scheduling.

Modern gardening techniques make possible the raising of a variety of healthful foods at home, with little need for pesticides, herbicides, or fertilizer. Heat storage and food-raising can be usefully combined, as shown in Chapter 8, The Garden of Eden. Growing food and careful shopping reduces incoming packaging. Recycling takes care of most of that, leaving only a few sacks of plastic instead of tons of potential landfill per year.

All of these strategies reduce imports into a home to the point where most needs can be met on-site, using commercially available, UL® approved equipment, for which progressive banks will grant loans. The added labor of gardening is often less than the labor needed to pay for store-bought food.

The exports—"house exhaust"—include heated, humid, possibly dirty air, "gray water" (mostly from washing), "black water" (urine and feces), and an array of "garbage." Health and ecological concerns insist that these be dealt with deliberately, preferably in a regenerative way, but always in a manner that does not bring grief to humans and ecological systems.

Exhaust air is not usually a problem, though a large number of air conditioners all running at once can add significant heat to the neighborhood or an entire metropolitan area, making the air conditioners work even harder. (Synergy can work in undesirable ways, too.) Wasted heat can have large-scale effects in winter as well: New Jersey ponds I skated upon as a boy haven't frozen solid for decades. City heat (all of it wasted energy) has changed the local climate. An autonomous house will cause or export little heat or airborne pollutants. A Dymaxion House would export even less, for it would need no paint, reroofing, or other resource-demanding, trash-producing maintenance.

Water polluted with chemicals and toxic material is a more serious problem. In rural areas, septic tanks and their leach fields are troublesome, and apt to contaminate streams, lakes, and groundwater. Urban sewer systems have similar problems on a larger scale. Both waste enormous quantities of pure drinking water to move small quantities of polluted water and toxic human wastes. Both are notably inefficient—dried in the sun, a year's worth of solid waste from one adult human will barely fill a pair of 5-gallon (19-liter) buckets! Low-flush toilets reduce water use, but still waste the waste. Bucky had a Dymaxion answer to this:

Packaging Toilets

Noting that pollution is valuable chemistry, in awkward concentrations, in the wrong place, at the wrong time, Bucky "decided to look at the plumbing"—something that no scientist had ever done. An autonomous Dymaxion House would not squander drinkable water to flush away the valuable chemistry that nature has designed us to excrete from time to time. Moreover, nature has separated that chemistry into liquid and solid—apparently for good reason.

Working with Don Moore, an experienced appliance engineer, Bucky designed a waterless Packaging Toilet that automatically and swiftly seals the excrement in plastic bags. Disease-carrying aerosols distributed by the usual flushing process are eliminated. A collection service picks up the bags for use as compost, feedstock for chemical processes, or as a source of fuel in the form of methane gas. Urine is caught and stored separately.

The packaging process is neat, clean, sanitary, and odor-free. It requires no piping, septic tanks, leach fields, or treatment plants. As population grows house by house, the packaging sanitation system automatically grows with it. Contrast this with the usual government bond issues requested for additional multimillion dollar facilities.

The Packaging Toilet has never been produced, probably because it is just one part of a whole system that must include an organization to collect and use the contents of the packages (a high-tech version of the traditional Asian "honeybucket" man). Public relations would need considerable work before the toilet and service would be widely accepted. Also, there was (and is) resistance from the large firms that build municipal sewage systems.

Infrastructure and marketing are an integral part of design, but Bucky was only interested in designing the hardware. The project stalled. Only astronauts have used an awkward, zero-gravity version of the basic concept. Back on Earth, the Packaging Toilet remains a logical, but unrealized, way to deal with septic wastes in houses, recreational vehicles, boats, and aircraft.

Fog Guns

The other major user (and thus polluter) of household water is washing. While in the Navy, Bucky had noticed that wind-driven fog kept the topsides of his ship—and his face—remarkably clean. It even cut grease. The "Fog Gun" is a device that uses a jet of compressed air mixed with a small amount of finely atomized water to blast the dirt off dishes, laundry, and, yes, people. For most purposes, no soap is needed.

An (allegedly) satisfying shower takes approximately a cup of water. I say allegedly, because I've never met anyone who has tried a commercial air-blast shower and liked it. (I don't either.) When confronted with this lack of enthusiasm, Bucky replied that *his* Fog Gun used a finer spray, and performed as claimed. In any case, the idea is certainly a good one, as it saves both water and energy. A bit of research and development should settle the argument, and might produce a useful product.

The two lower quarters of a 5-foot (1.5-meter) square Dymaxion Bathroom contain a sink and toilet at front and an oversize tub/shower at rear. Two matching, sealed "lid" sections (not shown)—one over the front section; one over the tub/shower—complete the assembly. Separated, the four lightweight pieces will fit through standard doors and stairwells for last-minute installation, or for retrofitting an existing building. Note the radiused corners that ease hygienic cleaning. The airliner ambience runs against the current irrational trend toward decadent bathroom opulence, but the Dymaxion is more efficient and sanitary, and dramatically less expensive.

Fig.2-11

The Dymaxion Bathroom

The Packaging Toilet and Fog Gun were intended to live in a Dymaxion Bathroom. A bathroom in a typical U.S. house is heavy enough to require extra structural bracing. It is usually made—slowly—from tile, with many hard-to-clean joints and crevices that can harbor dirt, scum, and disease germs. The multiple joints are prone to cracking, inviting water into critical areas where it rots the supporting structure or stains the ceiling below.

Construction is expensive. Remodeling is even more so. Each installation has to be custom-plumbed—usually in a way that makes access and repairs difficult without damaging something costly. Separate fixtures obstruct sanitary floor cleaning.

Molded plastic tub and shower enclosures are a bit easier to install and maintain, but they usually look like, and are sold as, cheap substitutes for the real thing. The sink and commode are unchanged.

The Dymaxion Bathroom is made as four rustproof, sheet metal stampings or plastic moldings, each small and light enough to be carried by two men up constricted stairways and through standard doors. This facilitates damage-preventing, last-minute installation, as well as retrofits of older buildings. The four components bolt together in a way that is permanently watertight (Fig. 2-11). Total weight: 250 pounds (113.4 kg).

The pre-plumbed sink, shower, and tub are built as integral parts of the room itself—a complete system rather than separate appliances. All corners and edges have at least 2-inch (5 cm) radii for easy swabbing. There are no cracks or crevices to catch gunk and germs. Electric heating strips in the sound-deadened walls keep the room warm and dry. A fan sucks downwards through a big opening below the sink, pulling steam and unpleasant fumes to the floor instead of past your nose. The mirror is mounted on the inside of the medicine cabinet door, where it remains free of condensation. The odorless, dry, Packaging Toilet needs no lid.

A partition containing the factory-installed, manifolded piping separates the tub-shower room from the sink and commode section, enabling two people to use the room at the same time. The tub is deep enough for therapeutic purposes and fun (you can float), yet its floor is raised high enough to make cleaning and child-washing possible without back strain.

The sink's nozzle is located in the rim nearest the user, directing splashes away from water-spottable clothes. Faucet handles are beside the basin, where they can be operated without reaching over or around a baby being bathed. Children raised in the Wichita House claimed the Dymaxion Bathroom was perfect for water fights—there was no way anything could be damaged. A floor drain eases mopping, and removes potential floods before they escape into the bedroom.

World War II interrupted the development of the Dymaxion Bathroom. Logically, the postwar housing boom should have provided a ready market for it. But indoor plumbing was available for the first time to thousands of GIs who had been raised on farms with outhouses. (In the 1930s, more than half of all Americans lived on farms.) The young war veterans and their new wives saw the advertisements for opulent, modern bathrooms. That's what they wanted, and that's what they bought. Dymaxion minimalism held no charms for people who wanted showy talismans against squalor. Today, bathrooms have become rather odd status symbols, disconnected psychologically, if not physically, from their function.

A German firm built a plastic version of the Dymaxion Bathroom for a while (minus the Fog Gun and the Packaging Toilet), but the idea never took hold with enough strength to change habits and codes. Perhaps single-parent, and two-parents-working families will come to realize how much of their lives is spent cleaning and paying for their "luxury" bathrooms. Maybe affordable, compact housing will need affordable, compact bathrooms. With a translation into new materials and techniques, the Dymaxion Bathroom would be just what many folks need. They'd be so cheap that each family member could have one. Now *that's* luxury!

It is not luxury, however, that is driving the change to autonomous buildings, it is practicality, convenience, and economy. Individual photovoltaic electrical systems are already cheaper than municipal power if the home is situated more than a half-mile (0.8 km) from the grid. A few composting toilets will now meet codes in some locations—a trend that is sure to improve as communities try to avoid the environmental problems and high cost of building new sewage treatment plants. There is a rapidly growing market in energy and water-efficient appliances.

The almost-autonomous house is well on the way to acceptance and availability on a large scale. The inefficient, expensive umbilical system of pipe and wire is sure to disappear, just as communication by wire is being replaced by wireless electronics. Only two major components need further work before true autonomy can be achieved: transportation, and the houses themselves. Autonomous neighborhoods and communities would solve the transportation problem by making most daily travel unnecessary. Grouped and located by need, preference, and region, they need not extend urban sprawl. Indeed, autonomy may encourage the tight, stable communities that so many people say they want, but are unable to find in tracts. Dymaxion autonomous house designs can provide the shelter. The technology is ready and waiting. We can build them today.

Fig. 2-12

Corrugated Cottages

Bucky was always alert for ways to bring a Dymaxion House to market in some form. If the time wasn't right for a deluxe model, then a humble one would have to do. It didn't need to wait for new materials or expensive tooling. It would be a start.

Galvanized steel bins like the one above are sold to keep grain safe from rats and weather. When Bucky encountered the bins for the first time along a Midwest highway in 1940, he immediately recognized them as the basis for an emergency housing unit that kept *people* safe from rats and weather. Sturdy, simple, watertight, and fireproof, the inexpensive bins were designed to be quickly and easily assembled by untrained farmers. Best of all, they were already mass-produced. Transforming a bin into a livable house would not require impossibly large expenditures for tooling costs, a problem that had doomed his much more complex Dymaxion House project a decade earlier.

Units were built from the top down by pulling the assembly up a temporary mast as parts were added at the bottom. The mast-hoist method kept most workers on the ground, speeding the work and reducing the risk of injuries. Bucky would use this top-down building tactic repeatedly in the future.

The original conical roof was replaced with compound-curved panels better able to withstand the mast-hoisting process, high winds, and blast concussion. The shadowless curves were also easier to camouflage. Deep corrugations added stiffness to the galvanized steel wall.

With the partially finished structure in this position, the interior of the not-yet-insulated steel structure became unexpectedly cool despite bright Kansas sun. Bucky was amazed to find that the heated air inside was going *downward* and out around the skirt while cool air came in at the top—just the opposite of what was expected. Thereafter, he often specified this natural "chilling machine" effect instead of air conditioning. (See section on "Chilled Domes" in Chapter 5).

Fig. 2-13

Fig. 2-14

The insulated interior of a 20-foot (6-meter) family version of the DDU was modestly, but comfortably furnished, as you see in this prototype. A heavy curtain room divider (shown retracted on the right) provided surprisingly good privacy. Doors could be installed anywhere to "marry" two or more units. Flooring was an unfastened gravity sandwich laid directly on the raised dirt contained by a brick perimeter ring. The bottom layer was galvanized corrugated metal. Next came felt insulation topped by Masonite® hardboard to give a solid, but rather springy, walking surface. Total DDU weight, furnished: 3200 pounds (1452 kg). Retail cost, furnished: about the same as a cheap car of that day (about $12,000 today).

Seed money came from Bucky's friend, Christopher Morley. The popular writer promised to support the project if his new novel, *Kitty Foyle*, was a success. It was. Kitty enabled Bucky to approach Butler Manufacturing Company, maker of the bin. Butler's enlightened president liked the idea, and quickly started development work. (Bucky always approached corporations from the top—an effective tactic.)

During World War II, Russian and American mechanics and airmen lived in these units in the Persian Gulf area while preparing to ferry aircraft to Russia behind Germany's back. Besides withstanding weather extremes, the tough metal construction offered a measure of protection from blast, fire, and shrapnel. Apparently, these domes did not take advantage of the chilling effect—they are a dark color, and no perimeter vents can be seen near the lower edge. The design was widely copied in the Middle East.

Fig. 2-15

This 1942 painting shows Butler products doing their part to win the war. DDUs are at left center. Patriotic publicity helped Bucky develop a reputation as a practical thinker, strengthening his connections to organizations with enough money to fund future projects.

Fig. 2-16

Like Bucky's DDU, this Integrated Living Systems experiment in autonomous housing is based on a steel structure already in production. Instead of grain bins, ILS director Robert Reines uses silo tops, which have all the advantages of true domes, but are not as strong as geodesic domes. Apparently, they don't need to be. (The same silo tops are commonly modified into astronomical observatories.) The "chilling machine" effect works well in these, keeping interiors about 15% below ambient summer outdoor temperatures whether or not the domes are insulated. Other than adjustable vent lids, no cooling devices are employed. Solar collectors and occupant activity keep interiors comfortable at subzero temperatures. The stone berm concentrates winter winds to sweep accumulated snow away from the dome. Bucky contributed a modest sum for the project's completion. Visiting Navajos like it a lot.

Fig 2-17

The time was right: World War II had started, and there was an immediate need to house radar crews in distant places with severe climates. The shelters would have to be delivered by air and installed quickly—possibly by illiterate workers. Bucky's modified grain bin fit the job description perfectly. Prototypes were successfully tested and approved. They got an official name: Dymaxion Deployment Units (DDU).

Always mindful of the value of good publicity, Bucky put a DDU in Hains Point Park in Washington, DC where various government agencies could handily assess its value and the validity of Fullerian logic. Another was displayed at the Museum of Modern Art in New York. When some spectators complained that it was a bit undersized, Bucky replied that a bigger shovel wasn't necessarily better; why should a bigger house be "better" than a small one? Like the shovel, the DDU was as big as it needed to be.

Bucky cut erection time by providing unenthusiastic assemblers with an incentive to open the next crate: an easily-stolen set of tools came with each house. Construction worker resistance to prefabricated buildings was a problem that would appear again, and would likely be a problem today. Getting code approval in each community, for each DDU, would also have been difficult. A civilian market seemed doubtful without substantial changes in the public image of low-cost housing.

Designers Michael and Ellen Jantzen fashioned this energy-efficient multi-dome home from a group of the same silo tops shown in Fig. 2-17. Interior shells are 24-foot (7.3-meter) diameter silo tops placed concentrically inside larger exterior ones, with the space in between filled with insulation. Silo tops are designed for one-day erection by two unskilled workers without a crane. The no-fasteners, slide-together "standing Chicago seams" add strength, do not depend on caulk for waterproofing, and cannot leak (Wet silage is a disaster). Finish is baked epoxy enamel over galvanized steel. Ingenious window shutters control light and privacy. Jantzen's clever joint between the domes prevents leaks and other problems caused by expansion and contraction. With an equally well-designed interior, the house has proved to be a good home after fifteen years in the northern Illinois climate.

Fig. 2-18

Fig. 2-19

Fortunately, building codes did not apply to the armed forces where performance (usually) comes first. The military successfully deployed several hundred units in the Pacific and the Persian Gulf areas. They worked well, but during a temporary steel shortage, the DDU was redesignated low-priority, and production ceased.

Meanwhile, drawings and models had been done for a prettier and more structurally efficient civilian DDU for use after the war. It was not a modified bin, but was designed from the outset to be a home. (In an emergency, it could be modified to be a grain bin—an interesting reversal of the original intent.) None were built. The project was cancelled—probably because the next move toward a true Dymaxion House was well under way in Bucky's mind. When the war ended, the lessons learned from grain bin architecture would be put to good use in the Dymaxion Dwelling Machine, popularly known as the "Wichita House."

Swords Into Plowshares

The 1946 Dymaxion Dwelling Machine, better known as the Wichita House, was the first true Dymaxion House. It took Bucky nineteen years of hard work to nurture the concept from scribble to "come-on-in-and-sit-down" reality. It had the potential to bring enormous social change. It didn't. But a modern version still could.

Do people pray for war? Few would admit it, but the end of World War II meant that thousands of war plant workers would join the flood of returning veterans seeking work. What would their work be? Grim memories of the Great Depression of the 1930s tempered the joy of approaching peace.

Peace also would end many wartime bureaucratic jobs, including Bucky's post as chief mechanical engineer at the U.S. Board of Economic Warfare. Far from being dismayed, however, he resigned a year before the war ended in order to avoid conflict-of-interest with his next venture, a marketable Dymaxion House. He had to move fast if it was to be ready when the soldiers came home.

The Dymaxion Deployment Unit (DDU) had worked well enough, but its summer camp amenities and barnyard aesthetic made it suitable only for wartime or emergency use. The civilian version looked somewhat better, but it certainly was not a Dymaxion House that would be suitable for marketing in the postwar world.

Fig. 2-20

The complete 36-foot (11-meter) diameter Wichita
House shipped in this container, designed to fit aircraft
cargo compartments and ordinary trucks. It weighed about
3 (2.7) tons. (A typical conventional house weighs about
150 (135) tons.) Sixteen inexperienced workers assembled
it in two days of cold, windy weather.

Bucky's new design was a round structure he dubbed the Dymaxion Dwelling Machine. It improved the 4D and Dymaxion Houses he had proposed—but hadn't built—sixteen years earlier. Like them, it was suspended from a single mast, and was stackable into multistory buildings resembling his earlier "10-deckers." Like them, it would pack small and erect quickly. But this time, the project would not stall for lack of capital and high-performance materials.

The war had brought the advanced metallurgy he needed just in time, and just as his graphs had predicted. The new house would take advantage of the strength and corrosion-resistance of the latest light alloys developed for military aircraft. It would be built on the same assembly lines, using the same workers, tools, and skills that were engaged in making warplanes.

After the war, the enterprise would simultaneously provide jobs and high-tech, affordable houses for returning veterans. It might even bring the archaic, fragmented housing industry into the future!

The Dymaxion car experience (see Chapter 4) had taught him not to expend his capital on a factory and tools. He would build no prototypes himself. Instead, the government would do it for the good of the country. Bucky presented the military with drawings for the "Airbarac" Dymaxion Dwelling Machine variously rigged as officer housing, barracks, and an "instant" multi-story hospital. (Figs 2-21, 2-22). The sophisticated structure had many advantages, but it was turned down for the same reason that the DDU project had been terminated: scarcity of materials. Then an unexpected turn of events caused the government to take another look.

Fear of German intercontinental ballistic missile attacks had forced new aircraft plants to be located in Wichita, Kansas, as far from the coasts as possible. The B29 bomber factories there ran nonstop, causing unpleasant, crowded living conditions for the three shifts of employees and their families. In 1944, with the end of the war in sight, many Beechcraft employees concluded that bomber-making did not have a peacetime future. Strategic bomber production goals were threatened when large numbers of workers began to leave for locations with more promising postwar job prospects. There was no legal way to stop them. Then someone remembered Bucky's proposed aluminum house.

Beech Aircraft's president, senior union officials (aircraft unions are used to rapid changes), and the government agreed that the Airbarac might provide an incentive for workers to stay. The Air Force ordered two prototypes. Work started immediately.

The single-mast design allowed military "Airbarac" Dymaxion Dwelling Machines to be raised above ground level or stacked as required. The 4-deck hospital version featured an outside gantry that delivered patients directly to the desired bed. Matching interior hardware lifted and turned patients, and handled heavy equipment. Five nurses could serve sixty beds.

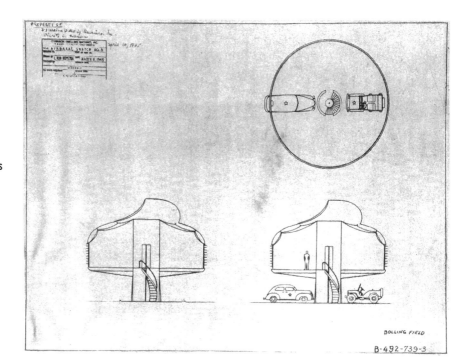

Fig. 2-21

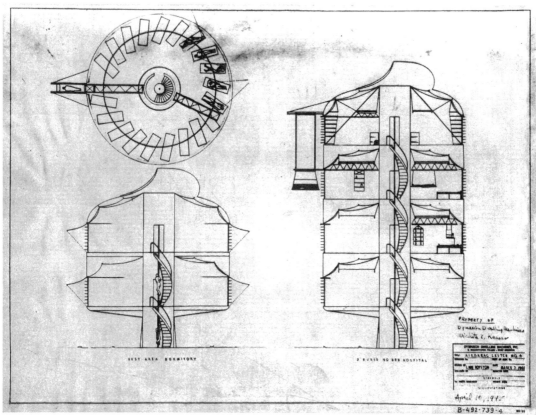

Fig. 2-22

Some of Beechcraft's finest aircraft designers, engineers, and craftsmen were assigned to the project. They were soon testing scale models in their wind tunnel, paying particular attention to thermal characteristics and the action of the hollow rudder-vent that would drive interior air circulation. (That ruddered vent had been specified 10 years before on the proposed Dymaxion Mobile Dormitory.)

Then came the full-scale prototypes. The aircraft-makers proved to be masters at producing small batches of precision components. The parts were stamped out with "soft" Kirksite (a tin alloy) dies that could be easily modified for the continuous upgrades considered normal in the airplane business. As work progressed, the exodus of workers stopped. But so did the war. The fledgling Dymaxion Dwelling Machine Corporation and Beechcraft were going to find out if swords-into-plowshares was a practical industrial metaphor.

Fig. 2-23

Fig. 2-24

A 10-pound (4.5-kg) sheet metal deck stamping is inspected for accuracy. Aircraft precision ensured that the house could be easily assembled, and would perform as specified. The 1075-square foot (100 square-meter) circular "deck" made up of these stampings could support 125,000 pounds (56,700 kg). The stampings also served as air ducts and heat exchangers.

A Beechcraft technician uses an inexpensive die to form experimental transparent panels for the rotating vent. The panels would have eliminated most need for daytime electric lighting, but no 1945 plastic proved suitable.

Bucky flips a "cowling gore" into place to check its fit on the full size pattern form. Most people would call the part a "roof panel," but to keep public perception of the Dymaxion Dwelling Machine clear, Bucky avoided the use of carpentry terms. No component weighed more than 10 pounds, permitting a worker to hold it with one hand while installing it with the other. Light parts were also easier and safer to handle. Most work was at ground level; like the DDU, the house was hauled up the mast as it was assembled.

Fig. 2-25

With all but one of the 96 gores in place, the cowling shows its shape. Gores are stretched tight by long bolts at their upper ends. The gaps between their edges are not fastened or caulked, permitting them to expand and contract without buckling. Water leaking through the unsealed gaps is caught by the chute-shaped ribs called "carlins." (Their tips are visible along the lower edge.) A circumferential gutter (not shown) collects water from the carlins and pipes it to collection tanks for later use. At night, circulating interior air is dehumidified as its moisture condenses on the underside of the cool, uninsulated cowling. The gutter catches that water, too.

Fig. 2-26

This mast base, mounted on a sunken concrete post, is the entire load-bearing "foundation" of the Wichita House. The only earthmoving necessary is to auger the post hole, a great advantage on uneven or environmentally sensitive sites. Steadied by X braces to the 12 anchors around the deck rim, the arrangement is virtually earthquake-proof. The house was designed and tested to support a live load on the floor equivalent to 500 large people!

Fig. 2-27

A jack and pressure gauge test the pullout resistance of one of the 12 earth-anchors spaced around the deck rim. In 1964, a tornado passed by only 300 yards (274 meters) away. It didn't damage the house, which was built to resist a total lifting force of 72 (66.5) tons. Home movies captured the event.

Fig. 2-28

Fig. 2-29

The Dymaxion Dwelling Machine Company vice-president, Cynthia Lacey rigging cable stays to stiffen the 16-foot (4.87-meter) bundled-tubing mast during indoor tests. Sailboats have used a similar tension-compression system for centuries.

The prototype Dymaxion Dwelling Machine represented the first time in history that aircraft technology—the most sophisticated available—had been applied to housing. The complete structure weighed about 3 (2.7) tons, and could retail for the same price as a luxury automobile (about 45,000 1996 dollars), just as Bucky had predicted.

It was intended to serve the same market as mobile homes, which today represent between a quarter and a half of new housing starts in some parts of the U.S.A. Dymaxion quality and performance, however, was vastly better. And, unlike its easily-demolished competition, it was specifically designed to resist Kansas tornados.

The low price meant that the house could be paid off like an automobile in five years instead of with a usurious thirty-year, high-interest-rate (about 250% today) mortgage. Two-day installation with minimal foundation work required no construction loan. Maintenance costs would be minimal—there was nothing to paint, nothing to rot, and no roofing to replace—again. Utilities and appliances could be upgraded as they became obsolete. Utility bills would be minimal, too; the low-drag, domelike shape retained heat well, and used natural air conditioning similar to the chilling effect first noted in the DDU.

The test house was first erected indoors, away from prying eyes and nasty weather. Its interior was mocked-up for publicity shots. The national media responded with a barrage of enthusiastic stories. Brochures were printed. Stock was offered, and it sold well. Visitors were first put off by the utterly unfamiliar giant-aluminum-hamburger appearance, but changed their minds when they stepped inside. They especially liked its light, elegant ambience and

Like a bulged bicycle wheel on its side, the cage of triangulated, adjustable tension rod "spokes" position the compression rings, and transfer the loads via the mast to the ground. The sheet metal skin, deck structure, and even the acrylic windows are in tension, too. The completed structure is strong, yet slightly resonant, like the wings of a large aircraft. After a few minutes, the odd boat-deck sensation is unnoticable.

Fig. 2-30

Fig. 2-32

A crude crane lifts the 18-foot (5.48-meter) diameter vent cap into place. The hollow rudder-vent rotates to keep its open tail downwind in the slightest breeze, sucking stale air from the interior. A similar vent is shown on the Dymaxion Mobile Dormitory (Fig. 2-10). If the low pressure area of a tornado passes nearby, the entire vent automatically rises 3 feet (0.9 meters) up the mast to spill interior pressure that could otherwise explode the house.

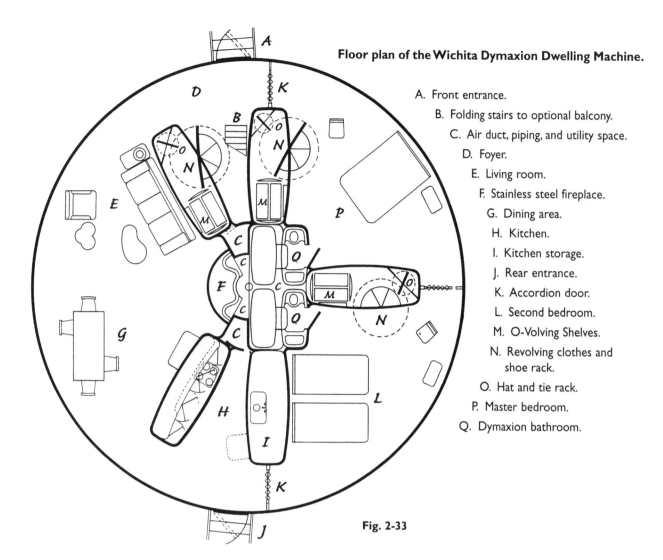

Floor plan of the Wichita Dymaxion Dwelling Machine.

A. Front entrance.

B. Folding stairs to optional balcony.

C. Air duct, piping, and utility space.

D. Foyer.

E. Living room.

F. Stainless steel fireplace.

G. Dining area.

H. Kitchen.

I. Kitchen storage.

J. Rear entrance.

K. Accordion door.

L. Second bedroom.

M. O-Volving Shelves.

N. Revolving clothes and shoe rack.

O. Hat and tie rack.

P. Master bedroom.

Q. Dymaxion bathroom.

Fig. 2-33

Fig. 2-31

"Potato chip" distortion of the top ring of the cowling disappears when all tension rods of the structural "cage" are tightened. The naturally occurring potato-chip effect was not a serious problem, but ordinary construction workers would have required special training. Bucky intended to use factory teams, a proposal that brought resistance from construction trade unions.

the low-maintenance design. Women noticed and appreciated the filtered air circulation and slick Dymaxion Bathrooms, which minimized housework. The company received about 3500 unsolicited orders—some with checks enclosed. (In his lectures, Bucky sometimes said it was 35,000 orders, but that number is not supported by office records.) In any case, public response was strongly positive.

With customers waiting, and a growing national enthusiasm for the idea, it was time to start selling houses. But Bucky stubbornly insisted that the house wasn't ready to sell. He pointed out that his 1927 prediction for the proper gestation of the Dymaxion House was twenty-five years, which would be 1952. He had seven years to go.

The stockholders and the board of directors were disgruntled. It was "time to shoot the engineers," as the saying goes. (If you don't, they will keep issuing change orders for improvements, and production will never begin.) Despite heavy pressure, Bucky remained intransigent. Once again, he was in danger of being fired by his own company. To prevent the marketing of an unperfected product, he "hid" the engineering drawings by stamping them "Obsolete." Perhaps they *were* obsolete; the prototype house that exists today differs noticeably from both those drawings and the patent drawings.

There were other problems obstructing successful marketing of the house: In many municipalities, only licensed union contractors can connect a building to city power, water, and sewage systems. Construction trade unions made it clear that they did not intend to hook up Dymaxion houses that had been pre-plumbed and pre-wired by aircraft machinist's union workers. Moreover, Dymaxion Dwelling Machines, Inc. had not yet developed the infrastructure of local dealers and trained installation crews that could have reduced such obstacles. That meant individual negotiations for each installation—an impossible situation made worse by antiquated codes that provided no way for building inspectors to deal with an aluminum house balanced on a mast—a house with a *rudder*, no less!

In the end, tooling costs turned out to be the biggest problem. The original agreement had specifically not included Beech paying for the tooling; they had new airplanes to finance. But banks will not easily loan money to enterprises with no dealers, union squabbles, and a divisive boardroom battle in progress. They also balk at lending mortgage money to the buyers of houses that do not meet codes, however antiquated. The banks all said no, and the project quickly collapsed.

Disgusted, Bucky swore he would never again engage in a business venture with money-making as its sole purpose. "You can either make money or you can make sense," he grumped. The experience had also taught him another lesson, one that he pointedly passed on to his students and apprentices: "*Never* show half-finished work." It's still good advice.

Bucky chats with opera star, Marian Anderson, in the living room. She deemed the acoustics excellent. The aluminized fabric ceiling helped to quell the echoes often found in round buildings. It also reflected radiant heat, diffused interior lighting, and deflected condensation drips. Bucky's many famous friends and acquaintances helped him gain access to high-level information sources and financing.

Fig. 2-34

This cutaway view of the model shows details of the living room and optional balcony. The curved stainless steel fireplace (center) was intended to soften the unfamiliar industrial ambience of the metal and vinyl interior. Room-dividing "pods" held revolving closets and O-Volving Shelves. The storage-wall pods can be easily shifted or removed (without demolition or construction) to make rooms bigger or smaller as desired.

Fig. 2-35

Bucky was tempted to furnish the Wichita House with radically modern, built-in pneumatic furniture, but board members insisted that the interior should be familiar to prospective buyers. Accordion doors took up less space, and could be motorized to open and shut automatically, reducing the spread of germs by doorknob contact.

Fig. 2-35

A touch of the button quickly brings the desired O-Volving Shelf (they're actually bins) to a single, chest-high opening in the wall, out of reach of small children. Think of the machine as two rows of accessible, floor-to-ceiling drawers. The idea has potential beyond mere use as a mechanized bureau: Bucky proposed that the entire collection of major libraries could be put on long, computer-directed O-Volving Shelf arrays reaching deep into basement repositories, eliminating vulnerable "stacks," and speeding book delivery.

Fig. 2-37

The spacious living room gave an impression of luxury reminiscent of a cruise ship or the first-class top deck lounge of a large airliner. It featured indirect lighting in a controllable choice of colors, and a 37-foot (11.3-meter) share of the encircling double-glazed, acrylic window. Just below the window, screened openings could be opened when extra ventilation was desired. With those openings closed, downdraft ventilation sucked dust into baseboard filters, reducing the need for vacuuming and dusting chores.

Fig. 2-38

The Wichita House Lives On

The Wichita House, as it had come to be called, was sold for one dollar to a visionary Wichita businessman, who rebuilt it on his land outside of town. (Fig. 2-43) It served as home for his six children, who liked living there despite water leaks and other annoyances. They reminisce about circumnavigating the round house entirely by crab-walking on the continuous interior windowsill, and driving adults crazy by "playing" the structure as a giant musical instrument, twanging the tension rods and thundering the high-tension sheet-metal-and-plywood floor.

Years of real-life use revealed problems, mostly caused by improper installation. The house leaked drastically (as it had been designed to do) because the contractor did not include the interior perimeter gutter to catch the water entering between the cowling gores (roof panels). Multiple layers of hideous (and futile) sealant marred the gleaming spaceship appearance (Fig 2-39).

The specified air-handling ductwork that would have provided solar heating and "chilling machine" cooling was not installed. In its place, a spiral staircase wound around the mast from the basement, through the main deck, up to plywood second-deck bedrooms. The rotating vent was de-ruddered and permanently immobilized to eliminate the rumbling noise it made as it turned, and because the kids worried (needlessly) about being sucked out. Without the intended air-handling system, conventional heating and cooling equipment ran up huge utility bills. When the owner died, the house was abandoned, and the family moved to town.

In the summer of 1992, I had the privilege of directing the dismantling of the Wichita House for restoration by the Henry Ford Museum & Greenfield Village in Dearborn, MI. We found that a colony of large, irreverent raccoons had enjoyed Dymaxion living for about fifteen years, thoroughly shredding and fouling the interior. Despite the mess, the place still had a hint of elegance. It was essentially whole and restorable. The worst damage was corrosion caused by animal urine and the use of common steel fasteners in aluminum. In contrast, the conventional addition had been irreparably damaged by rot and raccoon.

As we deconstructed the house (mostly by drilling out thousands of rivets), we looked for clues that would prove who was right—Bucky, or his board of directors. Was the house ready to market? The question was easily answered. We estimated that the house needed at least another year of development. If the missing air-handling ducts had, in fact, never been built and tested, even more time for experiments would have been necessary. Company records show no evidence of air handling hardware ever being made or tested full-scale. There was no sign of mounting brackets or holes indicating that it ever had been installed in this house. The Chronofile doesn't reveal how the chilling effect would have worked with the hollow rudder sucking air upward in opposition to the natural circulation patterns (see Fig. 5-4). Did the system work? The answer remains a mystery.

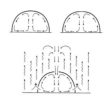

Many smaller, but nonetheless important details were not well worked out. Experienced prototype builders know that perfecting the details takes the most time. Some of the needed changes and refinements were trivial: The boominess of the slightly resilient floor could have been suppressed by the inflated rubber rug-underlayment Bucky had suggested for the 1927 Dymaxion House. Widening the impractically narrow exterior doors, however, would have required major changes; their odd contour was dictated by the position of essential tension rods in the walls.

The operable screened vents below the window strip had been riveted shut when their excessive flexibility made tight closure impossible. The remedy would have added a bit of weight, but was otherwise no challenge. A seemingly minor design detail was more serious: Since there are no solid interior walls, electrical outlets and switches had been installed horizontally in the window sill where they occasionally collected condensation (and leaks) running down the glazing. The resulting small electrical current leaks were potentially dangerous, and had hastened electrolytic corrosion between steel fasteners and the aluminum. That, too, could have been easily remedied.

Was the Wichita House a failure, as its critics claim? The Dymaxion deconstruction crew concluded that, with a bit more development, the Wichita House could have fulfilled its promise as a high-performance home. It is strong and roomy. The aesthetics—particularly inside—are much better than any of us had expected. Our only question is whether the house could have stayed warm with no insulation at all except for the radiant-heat-reflecting foil in the roof cowling. Perhaps that scheme would have worked as well as the counterintuitive chilling effect. The Chronofile and engineering reports are silent on the subject, possibly for good reason. Somebody should try it.

Fig 2-39

Fifteen years of occupation by a tribe of villainous raccoons left the Wichita House essentially intact while the conventional addition (foreground) had became an unrestorable wreck. Ineptly sealed roof cowl seams mark a futile attempt to correct leaks caused by installation without the specified water-collecting hardware. Despite the mess, the Dymaxion retained a surprising, if somewhat faded, elegance.

The last parts of the Wichita House base ring are removed for restoration, leaving a dreadful mess of trashed conventional basement materials to be buried. If the Dymaxion had been installed as designed, there would have been no wreckage at all. The house was not particularly suited to dismantling; thousands of rivets had to be carefully drilled out—a process that took six men four days. Separating the Wichita House from non-Dymaxion construction required another two weeks.

After forty-six years, many of the plywood floorboards had been delaminated by trapped spills accumulating along the edges of their aluminum retaining strips. Corrosive contaminants in the water ate the strips as well. A trivial change in the design (weep holes) or a different alloy would solve the problem. Proof-of-concept prototypes commonly have small details that need more work. Details can be surprisingly time-consuming.

Fig. 2-40

Fig. 2-41

The Dymaxion Dwelling Machine was originally intended as World War II United States Air Force officer housing, as you might guess from the sterile military look of this site model. Of course, civilian versions could have been landscaped as desired. A tract of these would look no more "all the same" than a tract of conventional homes. Needing no maintenance, the Dymaxions would always look neat. Their owners could be at the beach instead of painting shutters.

Fig. 2-42

The flaws in the Wichita House could have been caught sooner if Bucky had made the prototype himself, and lived in it when it was completed. His new policy of relegating development work to others made economic sense and left him more time for conceptual thinking, but it disconnected him from an important part of the design process. He knew that would happen again, but conceptual thinking came first.

As a concept, the Wichita House must be considered a success. It showed what was possible. It remains a wonderful demonstration of swords-into-plow-shares—"Killingry into Livingry", as Bucky liked to say. Today, the Wichita House concept represents an answer to the social disruption and political corruption caused by the closing of military bases made redundant by the end of the Cold War. The advantages of a Dymaxion House that were apparent after World War II are even more apparent now. A new project would bring high-tech, long-lived, energy-efficient housing at a price ordinary people can afford. It would be built by workers no longer employed in making weapons for a world that needs peace. Not a bad idea.

Bucky had it figured out 50 years ago.

Looking like an architect's model, the much-modified, privately-owned Wichita House perches on conventionally constructed basement rooms. Bucky mourned that the masonry addition "forever grounded this aeroplane." After restoration, this house will be displayed at the Henry Ford Museum & Greenfield Village Museum in Dearborn, MI. The grand opening is scheduled for 1998.

Fig. 2-43

Chapter 3
The Design Science Revolution

We are being taught. . . to assume as closely as possible the viewpoint, the patience, and the competence of God.—RBF

The Revolution

As it became clear to Bucky that political systems were incapable of reforming people in order to bring a good life to everyone, he announced a "design science revolution". Politics decides who gets to survive. Only by means of "comprehensive anticipatory design science" could the world's resources be fairly distributed among all people, and the need for war made obsolete.

Virtually no other designers were thinking that way at the time, and few are today. The environmental movement has focused attention on ecologically beneficial (or at least benign) design, but biology-based ecological designers tend to be suspicious of technology. Bucky did not claim to be a scientist, but he asserted that science-based, well-designed technology holds our only chance for survival. With it, we can "reform the environment [he meant the built environment] instead of people." What led Bucky to think that a design revolution could work?

He'd done his homework. By uncovering and analyzing the larger patterns in world commerce, and the rapid improvements in technology, Bucky concluded that there were plenty of resources if we didn't squander them on weapons and inefficient designs, or waste them on fripperies (made and marketed by his imaginary, multinational corporate nemesis, Obnoxico). In the 1960s, he sharpened his earlier inventory with numbers generated during his "World Design Science Decade", an effort to assess all the world's resources and know-how in detail. This was the start of the World Game, which carries on this accounting today. (See Chapter 10.)

With an inventory of available resources in hand, the next step for a designer is to use it well. Comprehensive anticipatory design science demands maximum overall efficiency with the least cost to society and ecology. Being comprehensive is a *direction* (Bucky called it "comprehensive prospecting") that implies extensive, omnidisciplinary research, a task recently made easier by the Internet. The goal is to optimize, rather than to compromise. Sacrifice, except in the heroic sense, should never be necessary. A well-designed product represents thousands of years of refined human experience.

Nature is not to be conquered or opposed, but she is to be regarded as a model of applied principles: Nature always does things in the most efficient and economical way. We need to learn how nature makes design decisions. The principles governing Universe have no exceptions, though in ignorance, humans often act as if they did. One of the startling things about the so-far-discovered principles is that they do not conflict with one another. Universe works as an harmonious system—incessantly regenerating as if it were the minimum perpetual motion machine. To be in tune with Universe, our designs should be regenerative. The current, overworked word 'sustainable' comes close.

Most design today is far too inefficient to be regenerative. Bucky's investigations showed that all of the world's rotating machinery operated at an overall efficiency of about 5%, a shameful figure that has not improved much since he first noted it in 1927. Today's automobile fleet, for example, is about 6% efficient overall. Out of every $100.00 spent on fuel, about $94.00 is wasted in various ways. Some of the waste is inherent in entropic physical processes, but there is enormous room for improvement.

That pathetic 6% efficiency is not the result of greedy plotting by auto and oil companies, it is the result of widespread ignorance. Few people think about their car's radiator, for example, a component engineered to throw away heat that their money just bought. Producing that heat also produced pollution. Both are waste. Waste is always a sign of poor design; pollution is a measure of inefficiency. The toll on consumer finances and the environment is enormous. Approximately 1% of humanity is scientists or engineers, and most of them are too specialized to understand the global effects of their work. The rest of humanity is technologically (and ecologically) illiterate.

Bucky figured that doubling the overall efficiency of all machinery would boost the world economy to the point where everyone could be assured of sufficient food, reliable shelter, and decent health care. This could be accomplished today without any new technologies. It is a matter of thinking comprehensively, plus encouraging and rewarding individual integrity that overcomes fear and greed. The dog-eat-dog lifestyle that degrades people and the environment is obsolete.

Naval experience and the information accumulating in his Chronofile, showed Bucky that technological advances most often derive from military requirements, or other conditions where high performance is necessary for survival. He noted that each round of improvements reduces the amount of materials required, and improves energy efficiency. (But pure science does not usually prosper during war; weapons employ the latest of what's already known.)

Military hardware eventually appears in civilian guise. Swords-into-plowshares, however, is a slow and costly way of going about things. If the same money and effort were put into civilian "plowshares" in the first place, the improved technology would become available to the general population much sooner, and without the middleman phase of inefficient, and often corrupt military contracts. There always seems to be enough tax money for the military development of a technology. If tax money is available for the military, tax money is there for civilian development. And the civilian goods can be sold. Military goods are in effect given away to the enemy, in the form of bombs, rockets, bullets, crashed aircraft, and so on.

And what of computers, and our much-touted, rapidly developing digital capabilities? In a private letter, Bucky wrote "… The importance of man in the next generation of technical research is very much greater than in the previous. The computer cannot ask an original question. The computer can only reask questions which were originally asked by the human brain. No computer can apprehend the plurality of potentially significant patterns newly emergent in evolution. Men will continue and flourish as the great question askers and exploratory inventors."

He also noted that "Development is programmable, but discovery is not programmable. Since the behaviors to be sought are unknown, computers cannot be instructed to watch out for them." He considered the term "discover" to be more accurate than "create." Bucky had been working on a computer design featuring geodesic architecture since 1964. Geodesics are by definition the shortest distance and least time between energy events. The patent drawings and descriptions, alas, are incomplete.

The anticipatory mandate of comprehensive anticipatory design science refers to looking ahead, taking into account the gestation rates of various technologies, and the time it takes to develop public acceptance. A designer should plan ahead in the same way a playwright prepares for opening night. Bucky's predictions were often right on schedule. When they weren't, it was usually because humanity behaved less well than he had hoped. He expected that designers and people acting as designers would become more comprehensive and scientific as know-how accumulated.

It is already happening, often inadvertently. Cities are reorienting to global air travel. Travel has gone from tracked to trackless as people take to the air. Satellites have advanced communication from wired to wireless. Photovoltaics and wind turbines can take the place of centralized power generating facilities for domestic electricity. Solar energy has reduced the need for piped fuel. Electronics and exotic alloys have taken technology from visible to invisible. Much mass has been replaced by information. Muscle is giving way to know-how and automation. But will the changes be large enough and in time?

Bucky didn't say. He resolutely refused the role of guru or prophet. (His editor and collaborator, E. J. Applewhite, tersely observed that "Prophets don't call themselves guinea pig.") If not a prophet, Bucky certainly was a missionary. Science fiction writer, Arthur C. Clark, remarked that Bucky may be our first engineer saint.

When pressed by this sort of accolade, Bucky would only claim to be a humble machinist, and produce his valid union card. When asked about the future, he said only that humanity had the resources and the know-how to make it a good one. Whether or not we do so is up to us.

High-Frequency Sleep and Odd Diets

The brain can only do its subconscious sorting when we are asleep.—RBF

Bucky not only lived his life as an experiment, he occasionally became a virtual guinea pig in his own laboratory. Extensive travel forced him into unfamiliar schedules of eating and sleeping. Obviously, this had not been a problem to previous generations of humans, who rarely traveled far, and could usually stop to eat or sleep as conditions required. Were sleep patterns unchangeably built into us, or could they be modified to fit the speed of modern life? If they were merely habit, he could train himself to sleep less. He'd have more time for work. He said, "Man as one being is awake and asleep, always two-thirds on duty."

A series of trials in 1932 and 1933 convinced him that feeling tired or sleepy was a sign that he had already overtaxed his body and mind to the point where they *had* to rest and recuperate. He decided to try deliberately sleeping before that point arrived. If he slept before pushing himself to exhaustion, repair and recuperation might not be necessary. Sleep would be for rest only. Perhaps it could be brief. If he kept to a certain routine, perhaps he would never be tired.

After trying many schemes, Bucky found a schedule that worked for him: He catnapped for approximately thirty minutes after each six hours of work; sooner if signaled by what he called "broken fixation of interest." It worked (for him). I can personally attest that many of his younger colleagues and students could not keep up with him. He never seemed to tire. His lectures could go on for ten hours or more. He seemed to be always scribbling notes, reading, making models, or just prowling around. The ability to keep going in that manner continued undiminished well into his 70s.

The Arthur D. Little research organization investigated what some newspaper reporters were calling "Dymaxion Sleep" after Bucky finally published it in 1944. (Bucky himself did not use the term Dymaxion Sleep.) They corroborated his findings, but noted that not everyone was able to train themselves to sleep on command. Bucky disconcerted observers by going to sleep in thirty seconds, as if he had thrown an Off switch in his head. It happened so quickly that it looked like he had had a seizure.

Catnapping was one of the tactics that enabled Bucky to accomplish an unbelievable amount of work in his lifetime, but critics noted that the technique could also be used to flog a workforce into higher productivity. It was thus not politically correct in a time of rising union strength. The critics were right.

Bucky's high-frequency sleep schedule has recently reappeared (without crediting Bucky) as "Power-Napping," a way of increasing executive productivity in the face of vicious competition.

Bucky never presented his sleep experiments (or any others) in a peer-reviewed scientific paper. As experimenter, subject, client and peer-reviewer, Bucky left himself open to accusations of unscientific conflict of interest. He answered that criticism by retorting that the results spoke for themselves. High-frequency sleep worked, though it was difficult to synchronize with the "normal" sleep patterns and working hours of others. There was nobody to complain, except his wife, Anne. She did. He went back to a more common schedule, but continued to catnap whenever he felt himself getting unreliable.

Diet and the timing of meals also interested him. To the dismay of vegetarians and environmentalists, he announced that meat was the best way for humans to get the protein and amino acids needed for good nutrition. Let cows concentrate the nutrients in grass for us. Cows can graze on land that is useless for anything else. Humans eat meat whenever they can get it. For much of the year, Innuit eat nothing but meat. We are designed to eat at the top of the food chain.

To prove his point, Bucky developed a diet consisting only of steak, prunes, Jell-o®, and strong tea, taken three, and sometimes four times a day, synchronized with his naps. He seemed to thrive on it, losing excess weight that had plagued him for years, yet continuing to demonstrate amazing stamina.

His doctors—and health problems he attributed to advancing age—returned him to a more conventional diet in the mid-1970s, about the same time that the true environmental and social costs of beef-raising were made clear. The research culminating in his *World Design Science Decade* books revealed much he had not known about food-raising and nutrition around the world. Always ready to take advantage of the latest knowledge, Bucky became an advocate of the winged bean, and revived his work on a Garden-of-Eden, food-raising Dymaxion home (see Chapter 8).

By the way, Bucky did not use drugs. He considered drugs (and the habitual addiction to mindless "entertainment") to be a plot to sap youthful outrage at political corruption. At one time a hard drinker, he quit using alcohol when he found people beginning to attribute his ideas to drink, instead of regarding him as a serious investigator.

I + I = 4.

With six identical struts, you can make two triangles. But when they are arranged synergetically, the same six struts make a tetrahedron of *four* triangles. There is a bonus: volume ("within-ness") divides Universe into what's inside the tetrahedron, what's outside it, plus a little bit that does the dividing. Nothing about the struts or the triangles hints at the enormous advantage gained by connecting them in this way. Only their relationship has been changed to bring about this efficiency. Bucky identified the tetrahedron as the minimum *system* in Universe.

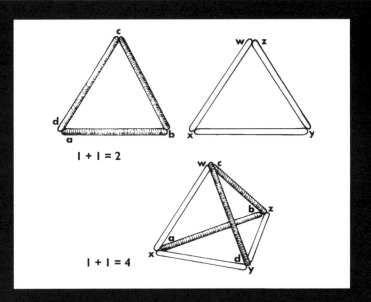

Fig. 3-1

Synergetics

"I have discovered the coordinates of Universe" —RBF

It took Bucky 1300 pages in *Synergetics* and *Synergetics 2* to present what he discovered (see Appendix A). This brief section is intended to encourage your further engagement in synergetics. It is a subject that will take time and considerable effort to comprehend, but if Bucky is right about discovering the coordinates of Universe, you'll be ahead of the pack. Even if Bucky's synergetics isn't right, or only partially right (most likely, since knowledge is always increasing in unexpected ways) you'll learn a lot on the quest.

"Synergy" is defined as the performance of the whole unpredicted by an examination of the parts or any subassembly of the parts. Bucky's favorite example was chrome nickel steel, an alloy that exhibits ten times the tensile strength of its weakest component and six times the tensile strength of the strongest. The tensile strength of the alloy is far greater than the *sum* of the tensile strengths of its components

Synergy also occurs in geometry (Fig. 3-1) and chemistry. After finding many examples, Bucky finally concluded that all of nature is synergetic.

The word "synergetic" is a weld of synergy and energetic. Energetic refers to energetic geometry. Because everything in Universe is constantly in motion, the Cartesian X Y Z coordinate system is incomplete; it does not take time into account. It is a way of thinking left over from flat-earth conceptioning. We are so accustomed to 90 degree coordinates that it is a surprise to see what we really mean by "squaring" and "cubing" (Figs. 3-2 through 3-6).

Bucky was very clear about this matter. In an address in 1965, he said, "In fact, experiment shows that we see and comprehend very little of the totality of motions. Therefore society tends to think statically and is always being surprised, often uncomfortably, sometimes fatally. Lacking dynamic apprehension it is difficult for humanity to get out of its static fixations and specifically to see great trends evolving."

Synergetics requires 60 degree coordinates. No insubstantial points, straight lines, or infinite planes are employed. Synergetic mathematics is based on experience rather than physically impossible axioms. Everything physical must have shape and structure. Bucky expected shape and structure would follow certain laws. Synergetics describes and models those laws. Like angles, they are unchanged by scale. In physics, synergetics explains the apparent paradox of electromagnetic phenomena being both wave and particle. In design, synergetics reduces or eliminates compromise.

In energetic geometry, a line represents a vector. It does not and cannot go to infinity because there isn't any infinity in regenerative scenario Universe. The line has length, angle, and an implied frequency. Time is always involved because real phenomena have duration. "*Time* is the shortest distance between two points."

Synergetics can physically model relationships with four or more dimensions, making them visibly comprehendible for the first time. Bucky regarded his geodesic domes as irrefutable pedagogical demonstrations of the correctness of his synergetic-energetic geometry.

Geodesics are synergetic. Nature often employs geodesic structure for maximum strength and protection. The eyeballs and testicles of some vertebrate animals (not all have been examined) exhibit geodesic patterns. Many tiny radiolaria are geodesic, enabling them to withstand deep sea pressures. Viruses are geodesic; Bucky expected that a study of their geometry would reveal how they work and how to combat them. Stacked tetrahedra form a double helix. Could DNA be usefully studied as synergetic phenomena?

The five regular polyhedra, or "Platonic" solids.

These are the only polyhedra with identical faces, and the same number of faces coming together at each vertex. If constructed of struts with unreinforced vertexes, only the tetrahedron, octahedron, and icosahedron are stable. This is not surprising, since the triangle is the only self-stabilizing shape, and these are the only regular polyhedra in which all faces are triangular.

The unfolded shapes can be reproduced, cut out, folded on the dotted lines, and taped together to make solid models. Refer to p. 243 for enlarged patterns.

Models made from soda straws with string running through them will reveal structural stability or lack of it.

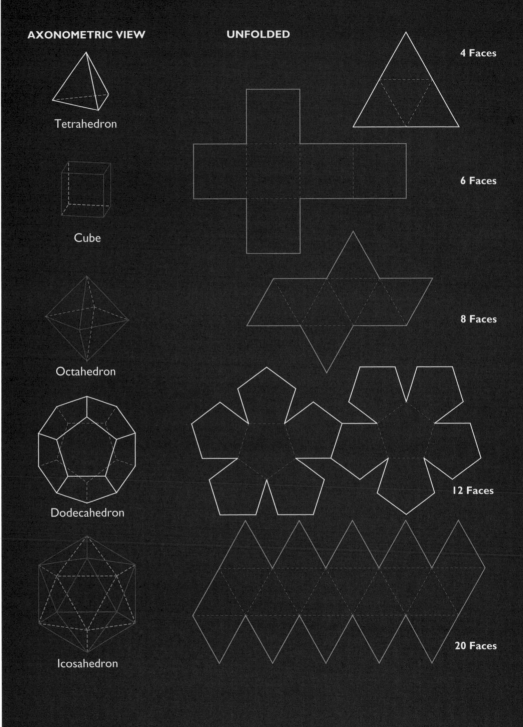

AXONOMETRIC VIEW

UNFOLDED

Tetrahedron

Cube

Octahedron

Dodecahedron

Icosahedron

4 Faces

6 Faces

8 Faces

12 Faces

20 Faces

Fig. 3-2

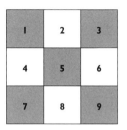

Fig. 3-3

When we "square" a number, we multiply it by itself. The multiplication is actually taking a number to the second power, but most people refer to squaring instead. Bucky considered this convention to be obsolete, because Universe is better described with a more economical 60 degree coordinate system than with the popular, 90 degree X, Y, Z coordinates. In this drawing, we see that "triangling" the number three achieves the same result as "squaring" it, but much more economically. A more descriptive term for either is "second powering."

Following the same logic as in "triangling", we see that "cubing", which is actually raising a number to the third power, can be modeled more economically as "tetrahedroning". Assuming a little tetrahedron to be the unit of volume, it is harder to see the total of twenty-seven in a 3X3X3 tetrahedron than in a 3X3X3 block of cubes. Here's how it works:

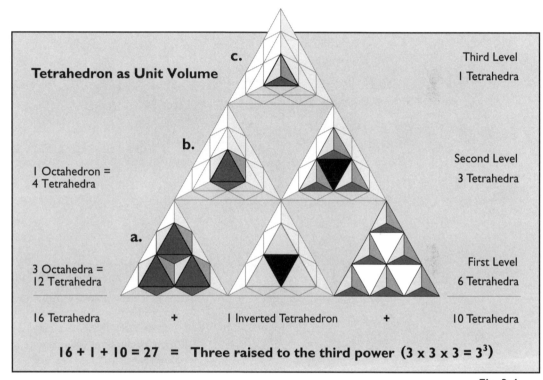

Tetrahedron as Unit Volume

c. Third Level
1 Tetrahedra

b. Second Level
3 Tetrahedra

1 Octahedron =
4 Tetrahedra

a. First Level
6 Tetrahedra

3 Octahedra =
12 Tetrahedra

16 Tetrahedra + 1 Inverted Tetrahedron + 10 Tetrahedra

$16 + 1 + 10 = 27 = $ **Three raised to the third power** $(3 \times 3 \times 3 = 3^3)$

Fig. 3-4

(a.) On the "ground floor" of the 3X3X3 tetrahedron there are six little tetrahedra (right), three octahedra (left) and one inverted tetrahedron nested in the middle. Each octahedron has a volume equal to four of the little tetrahedra. (For an explanation of why the octahedron has a volume of four tetra-hedra, see Figs. 3-5 and 3-6.) Thus the first layer has the equivalent of nineteen tetrahedra.

(b.) The second level has three tetrahedra (right) sitting on top of the three octahedra of the first level. One octahedron, sitting on the inverted tetrahedron in the first level, nests between them. Total volume is seven tetrahedra.

(c.) The third level consists of just one tetrahedron, giving a total volume of twenty-seven. Thus "tetrahedroning" is the same as "cubing" but is much more economical. A better term for both is "third powering."

(a.) Area of a triangle = one-half the base times the height.

(b.) "Shearing" a triangle along a line parallel to its base does not change the area because the base and height are not changed. Hence the areas of the three triangles shown are equal.

(c.) The volume of a tetrahedron = one-half the area of the base times the height. Shearing the tetrahedron does not change its volume because the height and the area of the base do not change.

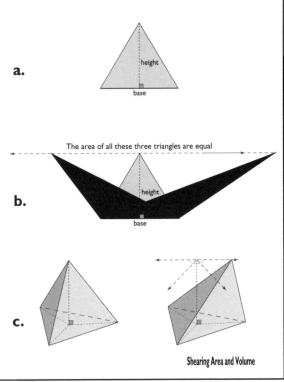

a.

b. The area of all these three triangles are equal

c. Shearing Area and Volume

Fig. 3-5

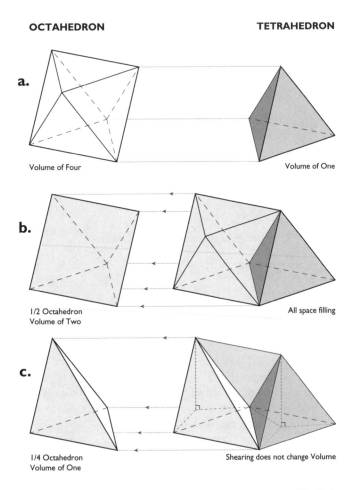

OCTAHEDRON   **TETRAHEDRON**

a.

Volume of Four   Volume of One

b.

1/2 Octahedron   All space filling
Volume of Two

c.

1/4 Octahedron   Shearing does not change Volume
Volume of One

Fig. 3-6

One octahedron equals four tetrahedra.

(a.) If a tetrahedron and an octahedron have the same edge lengths, they also have the same size triangular faces. If the tetrahedron is assigned a volume of one, the octahedron with identical faces must have a volume of four. Here's how it works.

(b.) On the right, you can see that the tetrahedron and the octahedron have the same base size and the same height. (They fit together to make an "octet truss.") Slice the octahedron in half and remove it (left).

(c.) Now remove half of that, leaving one-fourth of the octahedron. Because its base and height are the same as the tetrahedron, you can see that it is actually a sheared tetrahedron, and so must have the same volume. Thus, the octahedron has a volume of four tetrahedra.

Bucky went even further, saying that "understanding is symmetrically tetrahedronal"—a typical Fullerian sentence requiring some background and thought to comprehend. Indeed, the subtitle of his *Synergetics* books is "Explorations in the Geometry of Thinking."

The introduction above is just a taste of the complex, interrelated phenomena explained by a study of synergetics. Though there has been no organized effort to examine all disciplines for synergetic relationships, Bucky's ideas are beginning to show up more often.

The Octet Truss

I discovered that the tetrahedron was at the root of the matter. —RBF

The contest is to bridge a certain distance—two feet is usual—using nothing but toothpicks, sewing thread, and a bit of glue. The winning bridge is the one supporting the most red bricks with the least number of toothpicks. Once a favorite assignment for university freshman engineering students, the "bridge problem" is now common in high schools. Sometimes there are scholarships involved. An octet truss will win every time. I recently witnessed a 2-ounce (57 g) octet truss support 35 pounds (16 kg).

The octet truss consists of regular octahedra and tetrahedra, each with the same edge lengths, arrayed as a thick platform. They fit naturally (Fig. 3-6b). The octet arrangement is all-space-filling, as is an endless array of stacked cubes, but an octet truss is energetically three times more efficient than a cubic array. The octet truss is also triangulated in all directions. Cubes must have additional triangulating members to prevent collapse. This will be obvious if you make a model cube using soda straws laced together with thread running through the straws. Without reinforced corners, it is terminally floppy. An octet truss model will be stiff.

If you add a diagonal to stiffen each face of a cube, the diagonals will form a tetrahedron. Bucky reasoned that it would be more economical to start with a tetrahedron in the first place. But tetrahedra alone will not fill all space; they must have octahedra in between. Bucky's first commercial dome, the Ford Rotunda, consisted entirely of octet trusses arranged as triangles. (See Figs. 5-6 — 5-10). Octet trusses are mostly air, but are remarkably stiff, as the floors in the Windstar dome show (Fig. 8-30). Because it is triangulated in all directions, and does not depend on gravity for strength or integrity, octet geometry is often employed in space platforms and satellites.

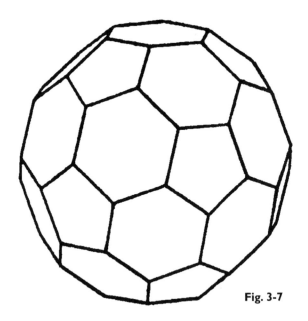

The 60-atom carbon molecule C_{60}, buckminsterfullerene, takes the shape of a soccer ball. The soccer ball pattern is a spherical icosahedron that has been "truncated." That is, the tips of each of the 12 pentagonal vertexes of the icosahedron have been snipped off to make 60 vertexes, all of which are equidistant from the center of the sphere.

Fig. 3-7

Buckminsterfullerene

Bucky did not discover, claim to discover, or even predict C_{60}, the remarkable carbon molecule that bears his name, but he did have an indirect hand in its recognition. A number of researchers had encountered the unusual, 60-atom carbon molecule in the early 1970s. A few suggested that it might have the soccer-ball pattern but none recognized the significance of what they had discovered. A decade later, Harry Kroto and Richard Smalley independently found C_{60} while looking for other molecules, and did recognize what they had. Both had visited the Montreal Expo dome (Fig. 8-21).

Merely looking at that huge icosahedral dome gave them a subconscious clue to what the molecule's shape might be. They looked at Marks' book, *The Dymaxion World of Buckminster Fuller* (see Appendix A), but it took some experiments with toothpicks stuck into Gummy Bear hubs to demonstrate that pentagons were necessary. (The pentagons on big domes are hard to spot.) Geodesic constructions must have pentagons if they are to close in on themselves to make a volume. A dome cannot be all hexagons. Hexagons would be flat, like a hex-tile floor.

The unusually stable C_{60} molecule was explained by the pentagon-hexagon pattern seen on a soccer ball (Fig. 3-7). That pattern has five-fold symmetry related to the icosahedron. If you "truncate" (slice off the tips) of the 12 pentagonal vertexes of an icosahedron, you end up with the soccer ball's pentagon-hexagon pattern, which has the necessary 60 vertexes. Kroto and Smalley eventually proved experimentally that the molecule did indeed have that shape.

They published their paper in 1985, two years after Bucky's death. In it, they named the molecule "buckminsterfullerene," acknowledging Bucky's work with geodesics. The lengthy name has been popularly corrupted to "buckyball." When Bucky's collaborator and editor, E. J. Applewhite, saw the paper, he sent the discoverers copies of Bucky's two *Synergetics* books which explain the mathematics and geometry involved in the icosahedron and its derivatives. Bucky also expounds at length on carbon and its tetrahedral bonds.

The story (so far) has been chronicled in *Perfect Symmetry: The Accidental Discovery of Buckminsterfullerene,* by Jim Baggot (1994, Oxford University Press), and *The Most Beautiful Molecule,* by Hugh Aldersey-Williams (1995, John Wiley). Mr. Applewhite continues to monitor and publish articles on the astonishing growth of the new branch of organic chemistry inspired by the discovery.

Tensegrity

There are no SOLIDS! There are no THINGS! —RBF

On stage, Bucky would bellow those claims in his most insistent voice. He contended that Universe consists of islands of compression in a sea of tension at any scale. Stars and planets are islands of compression in a sea of gravity. The moon is hooked to Earth by a weightless gravitational "cable" of zero section, yet of exactly the required strength. Atoms are relatively spaced as far from one another as the planets are from one another. In all of Universe, nothing is actually touching anything else. It's all energy, ordered by angle and frequency.

As usual, Bucky started with the biggest picture possible as he attempted to understand and explain the principles of structure. Any structure, any system, must have a shape. He was determined to find out why nature uses the shapes she does. Since nature always employs the most economical means, it seemed logical that we should too.

As a practical matter on Earth, tension and compression in buildings are handled by components such as cables and bricks. Steel beams, reinforced concrete, and wooden joists carry both compression and tension, but since tension is much more efficient than compression, Bucky preferred to have as much material as possible used in tension. He sought ways to make structures employing continuous tension and discontinuous compression, reflecting what nature was doing at macroscopic and microscopic scales. His student, Kenneth Snelson, made the first model demonstrating that this was possible (Fig. 3-8). Bucky called such structures tensional integrities, or "tensegrities."

As is true of all systems, a geodesic structure has a frequency (Fig. 3-9). As frequency increases, the compression members get smaller and smaller, finally becoming subvisible. This can be continued in a fractal manner (angles and proportions do not change with frequency) right down to atomic level, where the tensile elements are reduced to sectionless gravitational attraction. This is the basis for Bucky's remark that architecture is the art of making big structures from small structures. (See Fig. 6-12 for a tensegrity dome.)

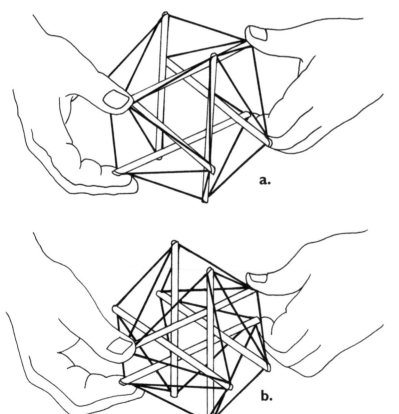

(a.) This model clearly demonstrates the principle of tensegrity. The rubber cord provides continuous tension that positions and maintains the shape defined by the six dowels. Like all tensegrities, this figure is resonant, behaving pneumatically as if it were a crude balloon. It is perfectly balanced—the short spans of rubber cord twang at the same note—and is remarkably resistant to permanent deformation. (You can make this model yourself from dowels with slitted tips, and identical rubber bands. It is also available as a kit from BFI, see Appendix B.)

(b.) When any two of the struts are squeezed together, the entire structure contracts uniformly and symmetrically, maintaining its topology and relationships. If the two struts are pried apart, the structure enlarges in the same way. When released, it will spring back to its original configuration. Tensegrities can take many shapes, including columns, spheres, and domes. Individual compression members can be replaced by higher frequency tensegrities, and those with still higher frequencies, until the structure becomes invisible and finally is down to atomic level. As this is done, strength increases!

Fig. 3-8

FRONT VIEW

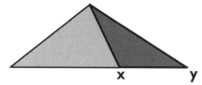 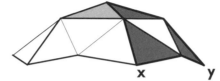 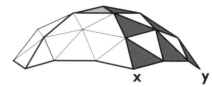

TOP VIEW

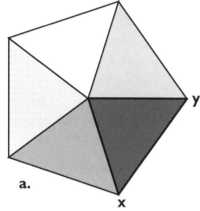 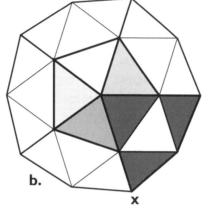 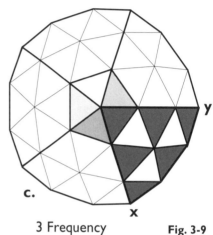

a. No Frequency

b. 2 Frequency

c. 3 Frequency

Fig. 3-9

By raising the "frequency" of an icosahedron, the edges of the big, flat triangles are subdivided into shorter segments and smaller triangles to make the icosahedron more spherical. All vertexes would touch the inner surface of an enclosing sphere. It makes no difference whether the structure is made of struts, facets, or is solid.

(a.) The side and top view of one of the twelve pentagons of an icosahedron.

(b.) In a two-frequency dome, each edge of one face of the icosahedron (darkest shading) is subdivided into two slightly longer segments, producing a new, bulged triangular face made up of four smaller triangles. The vertexes X and Y are actually the central vertexes of the neighboring pentagons. Bucky claimed that all real spheres are actually very high frequency icosahedra with tiny triangular facets. Calculating the volume of a faceted sphere does not require the use of the irrational (and annoying) pi.

(c.) In a three-frequency dome, the edges of the icosahedron are divided into three segments, producing a still more spherical, bulged face with nine triangles. The majority of small domes—up to about 40-foot (12-meter) diameter—are three-frequency (Fig. 8-22, for example). Again, X and Y are the center vertexes of the neighboring pentagons. In this type of dome, counting the number of struts between the center vertexes of any two pentagons will reveal the frequency. On a complex dome such as the big one at Montreal (Figs. 8-17, 8-21), the pentagons are hard to see, but they must be there.

He noted, however, that a study of the smaller structures does not hint at what bigger ones may be constructed from them. A look at one of Dr. Ingber's cells (discussed below) gives no clue as to whether the cell is from a gnat or an elephant. By starting with the basic principles of tensegrity instead of a product using it, Bucky gained an understanding of the natural laws involved. He was then able to apply them to special cases as a matter of design.

Dr. Ingber's Cells

Donald Ingber, M.D. saw his first simple tensegrity model while a student in a sculpture class at Yale in 1975. He was intrigued by the way that applied loads were transmitted almost instantly throughout the entire structure, deforming it without damage or changing its topology.

At the same time, he was culturing cells in a laboratory course. In a moment of serendipitous recognition, he noticed that the cells and the tensegrity model behaved in a similar way under load. In both cells and the tensegrity, the relationships and topology remain intact despite distortion. Could the architecture of cells be a tensegrity? If so, could that arrangement influence cell functions?

Subsequent experiments and analysis by Dr. Ingber and his associates suggest that the cytoskeleton—the "scaffolding" in cells—does take the form of a complex tensegrity with thousands of discontinuous compression members ordered and stabilized by continuous internal tension filaments. It seems likely that the nucleus is structured in the same way (Fig. 3-10). Such a system maintains its integrity without relying on gravity. By (almost) instantly distributing applied loads, it can act as a transducer, a receptor, and carrier of information that regulates cell behavior.

Bucky maintained that Universe, when viewed at any scale from galaxies to atoms, is made up of islands of compression in a continuous sea of tension. He insisted that nature had to utilize tensegrity containment because it is the most economical use of material. It is not surprising that he thought highly of Dr. Ingber's pioneering work.

Dr. Ingber published a detailed paper in *Journal of Cell Science* (Volume 104, pp. 613-627, 1993) called "Cellular Tensegrity: Defining New Rules of Biological Design that Govern the Cytoskeleton." Another paper, "Mechanotransduction Across the Cell Surface and Through the Cytoskeleton," appeared in *Science* (Volume 260, 21 May 1993). He can be reached by e-mail: ingber_d@a1.tch.harvard.edu

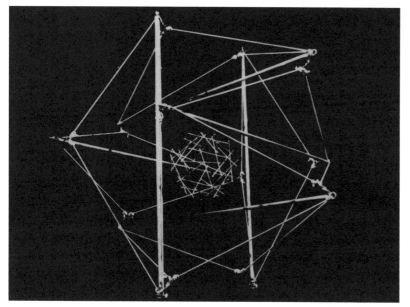

(a.) Dr. Ingber's tensegrity model of simplified cell structure with its nucleus, itself a tensegrity sphere. The struts of the cell model are connected by continuous elastic cord, as are the struts of the nucleus. For clarity, the cell and the nucleus are connected in tension by black elastic thread, made invisible against the black background in this photograph to reduce visual confusion. This tensegrity model represents the cell and nucleus as omnisymmetrical, roughly spherical shapes, maintained by the internal tension of the elastic cords. A living cell has thousands of compression "struts" and tension filaments.

a.

(b.) The tensegrity cell model distorted and anchored to a firm substrate. The nucleus has distorted in concert with the cell to which it is connected, and has also dropped to the substrate. If released, the cell and nucleus will spring back to their original spherical state. Note that the relationships and topology have not changed as the cell shape is manipulated.

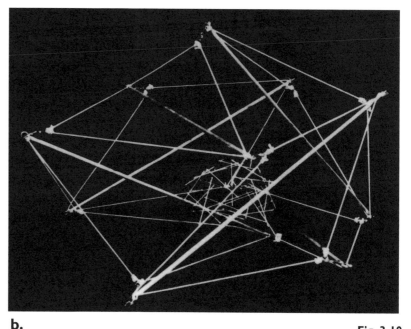

b.

Fig. 3-10

Was Bucky Right?

Laws require proof.
Synergetic principles and theories
Thus far described
have been experimentally demonstrated;
Their concurrent mathematical proof
Is the work of others. —RBF

Does synergetics describe the coordinates of Universe? That's the Big Bucky Question. As a student in the 1950s, I could not understand why mainstream scientists neither derided nor applauded Bucky's concept of synergetics. If he was wrong, disproving his unconventional notions should have been easy. If he was right, why weren't his ideas being used and taught? My professors resolutely dodged the question. Most refused to discuss Fuller at all. At the time, I thought they were avoiding discussion until they had familiarized themselves with his ideas. It's been forty years. I'm still waiting.

Attacks from academe would be easier to understand than refusal to debate. Scientists have a history of savaging upstarts. At about the same time Bucky began to promulgate his energetic/synergetic geometry (later shortened to "synergetics"), Immanuel Velikovsky's *Worlds in Collision* (1950, Doubleday) drew heavy fire for citing archaeological, geological, and anthropological evidence to dispute establishment astronomers. A few famous names were so incensed that they noisily (and rather unscientifically) denounced the book without reading it. Velikovsky was not permitted to reply in peer-reviewed science publications. Few scientists dared agree publicly with anything Velikovsky said, for fear of committing professional suicide.

Bucky's concept of synergetics was more deeply radical and much more comprehensive than Velikovsky's hubristic, turf-invading proposals, yet Bucky was not, and has not, been either attacked or vindicated by the scientific establishment. A handful of critics have sniped at his chemistry, or indicated a lack of respect for the inconsistencies (there are many) and occasionally fuzzy details in his seminal *Synergtics* books, but none have mounted an orchestrated assault on his major claims.

Fullerphiles suggest that the silence is induced by fear. If Bucky is right about nature using a 60-degree coordinate system, the Cartesian 90-degree X Y Z coordinate system is mistaken or incomplete, however useful it may be. To bring that into public focus would be too confusing and destructive, not to say embarrassing.

Another explanation is that overspecialization has bred a science community devoid of scholars with expertise sufficiently broad to mount a credible critique of Bucky's comprehensive metaphysics. Moreover, unsupported hostility might be dangerous: Bucky had some powerful scientist allies. Among them were Jonas Salk and Linus Pauling—both experienced in dealing with self-induced controversy.

Fullerphobes dismiss him as a pseudoscientist, a more damning label than being deemed incompetent. He was not worth the trouble of disproving. Why even discuss his mathematics when he had no advanced degree in mathematics? In fact, he had no degree at all. (In this sort of argument, his 47 honorary doctorates don't count.) Specialists want no part of dilettantes.

With no "license" in a specialty, Bucky was regarded as a "generalist", a polite term for persons with no real expertise. Generalists know a little bit about a lot of things. They tend to generalize to the point where credibility is lost. Regrettably, Bucky sometimes used "generalist" himself, when "comprehensivist" would have been more accurate. Comprehensivists concentrate, as he did, not just on things, but on connections and relationships. He certainly was an expert at that, but comprehensive analysis remains a discipline that is not yet widely understood or taught.

Bucky also was ignored, or taken for a crackpot because he seriously investigated phenomena considered to be suspect by most scientists. For instance, he openly studied and reported on numerology, thinking that "… it might contain very important bases for understanding new properties of mathematics." The chapter on numerology in *Synergetics 2* features some legitimate mathematical discoveries that he probably could have published in a journal, but he spurned peer review. His said his domes were adequate proof of the power of his mathematics and synergetic conceptualizing.

Bucky further discomfited scientists by daring to dispute Darwin, telling listeners that "We arrived from elsewhere in Universe as complete human beings." He suggested that apes are degenerate humans, examples of devolution instead of being our ancestors. Audiences of scientists were aghast (or politely amused) when he exclaimed, "If gymnasts only married gymnasts, we'd come to monkeys very quickly."

He suggested that dolphins evolved from the first Earthians in their first home—which he insisted was Polynesia, not Africa. Polynesians swam and dove a lot. Over millions of years, some of them became extraordinarily good at it. He chose Polynesia because the first humans on Earth would have been landed where mild weather, abundant resources, and no dangerous land animals made it easiest to survive without know-how. Later, forced to learn seamanship and navigation, islanders were better fitted than land people to explore and populate the rest of the planet.

More controversy: Bucky explained that the decline of the family as the basic social unit, and the concurrent increase of homosexuality, and (especially) bisexuality, were natural evolutionary developments in a species that no longer needs a high rate of reproduction. For the same reasons, he expected that recreational sex will continue to increase. He said that these changes are not good or bad, and it is futile to waste time opposing them. Animals instinctively and genetically adjust their procreative activities in ways appropriate to prevailing conditions.

Perhaps most unacceptable to many serious scientists is that Bucky openly celebrated metaphysics, and the existence of God as the cosmic designer. Not an anthropomorphic God—more of a Divine Intelligence or Integrity—but God nonetheless. In his book *Critical Path*, he claims that his version of the Lord's Prayer "constitutes a scientifically meticulous, direct-experience-based proof of God." That sort of claim guarantees a hostile reaction, and undermines the scientific credibility of his other ideas. His denouncement of religion ("The next most dangerous thing to the atomic bomb is organized religion.") failed to deflect such criticism, while assuring the hostility of conservative clerics, politicians, and school boards.

These opinions, along with a famous outdoor lecture he gave to a group of several thousand "hippies" in San Francisco's Golden Gate Park in the 1960s, caused political conservatives to regard him as a left-wing radical despite his avowed aversion to any political party, pole, or posture. The geodesic domes seen in many counterculture communes reinforced that impression, which even today hinders their acceptance by building inspectors and mortgage lenders. Bucky's stint as lecturer for Werner Erhard's est sessions didn't help matters, and further sullied his reputation among scientists who didn't appreciate Mr. Erhard. (When directly asked, Bucky stated firmly that he had not taken est training, and did not make use of est teachings, but he did think Erhard was a "good human being.")

In another camp, Bucky irritated environmentalists by denouncing the Club of Rome's popular book, *Limits to Growth*. (Donella Meadows et al, 1972, Universe) He correctly asserted that the book was fatally flawed because it ignored recycling, regeneration, and humanity's ability to learn and improve. He insisted that the worrisome conclusions were a classic example of sophisticated computer analysis gone awry because of flawed input and the deplorably narrow experience of the investigators. The authors eventually agreed that he was right, but environmentalists had already idolized the book as proof of impending doom brought on by wicked technocrats—such as Bucky. They didn't want to hear anything that would weaken arguments based on the book's grim outlook.

Biologically educated environmentalists were ambivalent about Bucky; not many understood that his mathematics and technology could help. Some attacked without doing their homework: A famous nature photographer accused him of "covering his formerly pristine island with technology" when, in fact, the Fuller family's Bear Island, off Camden, ME, had no electricity or running water, and the main house had an outhouse out back.

He has annoyed feminists, too. Some do not appreciate his views on the difference between the sexes: "Man is discontinuous, he comes and goes. She carries the eggs, and so is continuous, like tension. She tends to stay with the young and the old. She is the consolidator of gains brought in by the male, deciding whether to feed it, skin it, milk it, ride it, or eat it. She was the first to industrialize."

Every one of his major projects had a strong woman present as it gathered momentum, and her role was important. If few women were to be seen later in the "man's world" of construction, that was just how things were done in his day. There is no question that he regarded males and females equally when he spoke of education and our duties as humans in Universe. And through it all, his wife, Anne, backed him and supported him—a very difficult part to play. He died beside her sickbed. She died a day later, without waking. They had been together 66 years.

The foregoing is not intended as an apologia for Bucky's flaws, foibles, and unproved exploratory suggestions. His ideas are not always easy to understand. His writings are not always consistent, especially to readers who expect his early ideas to remain unchanged as he learned. He spoke to a lay audience as an integrator. There *is* an internal consistency to synergetics. If the basic premises of synergetics are true, Bucky's sometimes strange, always bold, assertions may also be true, for they follow logically.

There appears to be an enormous potential for more important discoveries of principles and connections in the study of synergetics. Though riddled with fuzzy details, Bucky's systematic investigations were, like all science, edging toward truth. Physical manifestations of his discoveries have worked well. His concepts need to be rigorously tested by the usual scientific means. If synergetics withstand comprehensive scrutiny (piecemeal examination of details out of context, and quibbling over minor details won't do), then synergetics should be widely taught and applied.

Chapter 4

Getting Around

Bucky's Dymaxion Transport projects had the frustrations, defeats, and victories typical of any bold move into unknown territory. The Chronofile reveals how the ideas evolved. You can sense Bucky's mind at work as he struggles to bring a metaphysical concept into physical reality. You can see why so many less daring designers play safe and cling to the past.

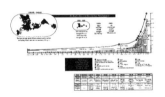

Ultimately, it had to fly. An early version of Bucky's graph (Fig.10-1), based on information in the Chronofile, showed that people were travelling faster and further every year—a trend that was accelerating as we become a "one-town world". If autonomous Dymaxion houses and 10-deckers could be zeppelined to almost anywhere on earth, their occupants and service crews would surely come and go by air.

Land travelers must pay for the construction, maintenance, and use of roads and tracks—the other half of all wheeled vehicles. But the sea is free, and you needn't buy sky to fly.

Trackless travel maximizes the choice of destinations. Much livable land is not accessible by road or even by misnamed "off-road vehicles." (A waist-high obstacle will stop any of them.) Ships can range at will over the sea, but navigable waters, canals (boat roads) and ports are limited, and the open sea isn't usually considered a destination. Only aircraft can go from anywhere to

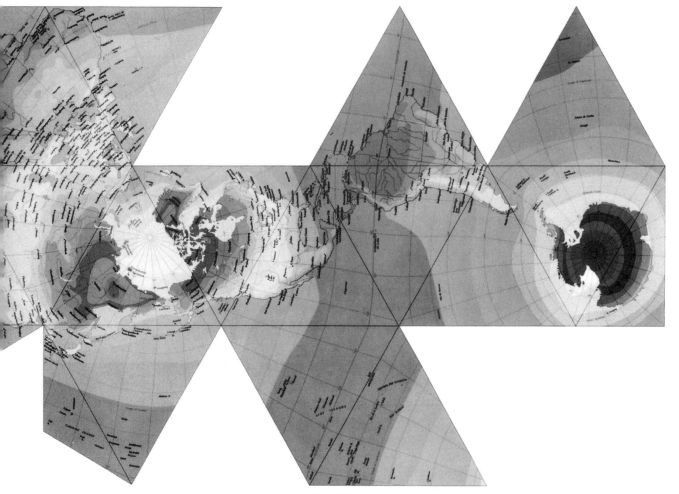

Fig. 4-1

The Dymaxion Map

The Dymaxion Projection map is the only flat map that shows Earth's land masses in their true contour and proportion. Distortion is minimal, and occurs in the oceans. Unlike a globe, it allows you to see the entire Earth at a glance. (Your eye can only take in one-fourth of a globe at one time. Try it.) The pattern is an unhinged icosahedron, and can be folded into that solid figure. The panels can be arranged as desired. The arrangement shown shows that there is actually one large land mass. Air travel routes over the pole are obviously the shortest great circle way to connect cities in the northern hemisphere where most humans live.

Details of the projection method are shown in *The Dymaxion World of Buckminster Fuller,* by Robert Marks (1960, Reinhold). Maps are available from the Buckminster Fuller Institute (see Appendix B).

everywhere by the shortest route, encouraging decentralization and all manner of global synergetic advantage.

Flying is also more efficient than automobiling *as a system*. Bucky estimated that at any given moment, millions of vehicles were getting zero miles per gallon while waiting at traffic signals. "Think of two-hundred million horses jumping up and down going nowhere," he'd say, shaking his head at the sheer stupidity of it. A Dymaxion Transport could fly straight to its goal without pause. (Bucky had not yet thought about the urban sprawl his transports would make possible. In fact, he considered easy access to suburbia to be a desirable attribute of his machines. Dymaxion Transport would make cities—"warehouses for people and goods"—obsolete.)

Always alert to the principles at work in nature's designs, Bucky had noticed that ducks are held aloft and continuously fall forward on the bursts of air emitted by the rapid strokes of their stubby wings. About 1930, he proposed what we would now call a "jump-jet" or VERTOL (for Vertical Takeoff and Landing). The wingless "omnimedium plummeting device" was to be lofted by two swiveled "jet stilts," one on each side, angled slightly outward for stability. They'd pivot back a bit for forward motion, and forward for braking—like a duck's wings.

Bucky specified jets because they are smaller, lighter, simpler, and about four times more efficient than piston engines. No practical jets had yet been built, but Bucky's graph showed that they'd come in a decade or so—which they did. Bucky could afford to wait. He knew that all ideas have their natural gestation rate. Meantime, the landing gear could be developed for "prolonged taxiing" (his hopeful term for driving) and safe crosswind behavior on roads and rough ground.

Bucky certainly did not start out to design an automobile. Three wheels made the most sense as a landing gear—a fourth is not needed for support, adds weight and drag, and tends to make a vehicle rock like a four-legged chair on an uneven floor. She'd steer from the back "like a bird or a fish," and be outrageously maneuverable. The single rear wheel would permit an aerodynamically efficient shape in both plan and profile (Fig. 4-4).

Bucky finally settled for a grounded rear wheel, and 75% of the weight on the driven front axle to ensure traction and stability—and good balance as an aircraft. The center of gravity was a dramatically low 23 inches (58.4 cm), about the same as today's cars (Fig. 4-2).

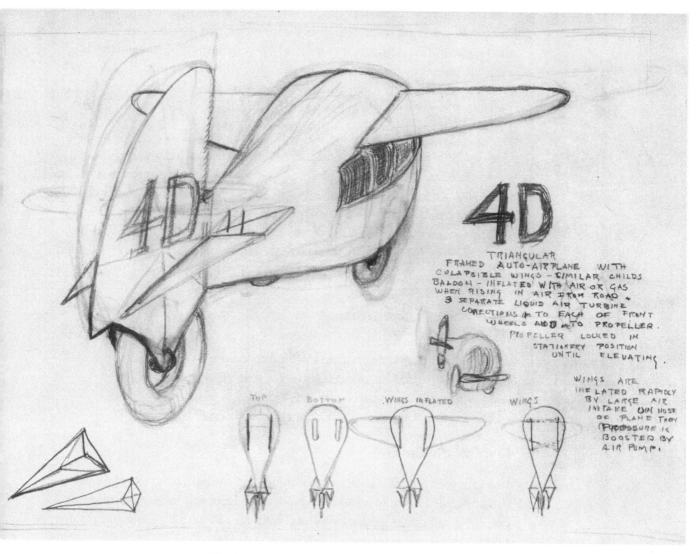

4D

TRIANGULAR FRAMED AUTO-AIRPLANE WITH COLAPSIBLE WINGS – SIMILAR CHILDS BALOON – INFLATED WITH AIR OR GAS WHEN RISING IN AIR FROM ROAD. 3 SEPARATE LIQUID AIR TURBINE CONECTIONS ⅟ TO EACH OF FRONT WHEELS AND ⅟ TO PROPELLER. PROPELLER LOCKED IN STATIONERY POSITION UNTIL ELEVATING.

WINGS ARE INFLATED RAPIDLY BY LARGE AIR INTAKE ON NOSE OF PLANE THEY (PRESSURE IS BOOSTED BY AIR PUMP.

TOP   BOTTOM   WINGS INFLATED   WINGS

Fig. 4-2

The first 1927 4D Transport sketch is this personal airplane that could be used as an awkward automobile when the inflatable wings were stowed. It would need minimal space for takeoffs and landings, but even that seemed too restrictive to Bucky. That, and the goose-like clumsiness on the ground caused him to seek other solutions.

Conventional cars were heavy then—everyone "knew" that weight was needed to hold the road and to provide a comfortable ride. (Neither claim is true.) But the Dymaxion Transport had to be light—after all, she'd be flying someday. Aerodynamics took precedence over styling. Think how absurd aircraft would be if they flaunted the ostentation of a royal carriage—as luxury cars did then—and attempted to gain prestige by stuffing a chromed replica of the Parthenon through the air—as Rolls-Royce did, and still does.

Bucky didn't respect auto stylists; their contemptible mission was to make things *look* new without *being* new. He was not the only one interested in aerodynamics. The American designer Norman bel-Geddes and a number of Europeans were working on low-drag designs. Aircraft designer William Stout had his appropriately-named Scarab car on the road. Competition didn't bother Bucky: "Evolution makes many starts" he said. Besides, only his was intended to fly someday.

Dymaxion Plummeting

The reason I built an advanced design car rather than an advanced design house was simply because I knew I could draw on the already available inventory of parts from the automotive world. There was nothing like that available for housing.—RBF

Dymaxion Cars

In 1933, with a logical design in hand (and no computers for simulations), Bucky decided to build a full-scale proof-of-concept machine. An astute financial move had preserved his cash from failing banks, and his enthusiasm for building a better future had attracted several investors, including a stockbroker and an aviatrix contemporary of Amelia Earhart.

He hired six world-class craftsmen out of a thousand hungry applicants. For chief engineer, he appointed Starling Burgess, famous for his high-performance seaplanes and America's Cup racing yachts. Bucky had high regard for Burgess, who had done the calculations for the 4D tower's streamlined fairing (Fig. 2-5), and the central mast of the proposed Dymaxion House.

Work commenced in 1933, on the very day that President Franklin D. Roosevelt announced the infamous bank moratorium—perhaps the worst moment of the Great Depression. It took the inspired crew just six weeks to produce a chassis ready for road testing (Fig.4-5).

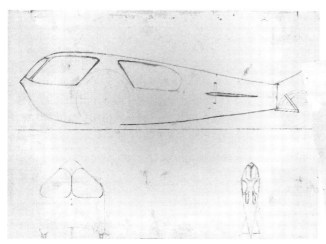

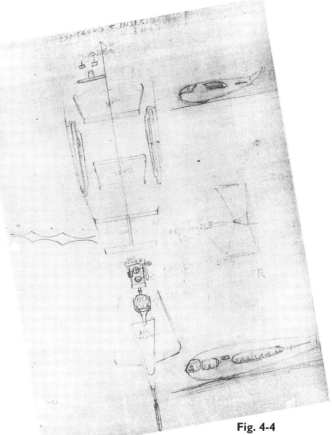

Fig. 4-3

Early drawings show the tail wheel planing completely off
the ground, giving a ride-smoothing infinite wheelbase at high
speeds. In planing mode, steering duties were assigned to an
air rudder, and stability to the inverted-V "air keel" contour of
the belly fairing. Impractical, but there is much to be learned
by considering all options, including extremes.

Fig. 4-4

Eight men built this test
chassis in just six weeks!
It generally worked well, but
the simple layout let the rear
wheel lean with the body in a
turn while the front wheels
remained perpendicular to
the road. Correcting the
resulting evil gyroscopic
effects required the entirely
new, more complex design
used in the first complete car.

Fig. 4-5

Burgess showed considerable courage driving the naked chassis fast for the first time. Little was known about vehicle dynamics in general—certainly not enough to predict the handling characteristics of a three-wheeler with rear-engine, rear-wheel steering and front-wheel drive. The machine showed promise, but Burgess had some scary moments with uncontrollable steering oscillations similar to the "death wobble" rightly feared by motorcyclists and the drivers of trailer-towing autos. The remedy was time-consuming and expensive: Start over with a new chassis that kept all three wheels always perpendicular to the road.

Bucky did not view the need for a new chassis as a setback. There was no body of knowledge for reference, no experts to ask. Mistakes and dead-ends are common in research-and-development work, especially when an entire concept is new and not just a refinement of a portion of an established design. Learning always involves trial and error. Also, Bucky knew that it usually takes three tries to develop a convincing prototype. The first try shows whether the idea has promise; the bare chassis had confirmed that the idea was basically good. The next try would be the first complete car (Fig. 4-7).

The second prototype of a design is a version of the first, with the major flaws corrected. Work started on a wood-framed, aluminum-clad body utilizing the latest yacht and aircraft technology. There was a deadline: The first complete car had to be ready for the 1933 Chicago World's Fair in three months. The crew immediately grew to twenty-eight, including two sheet metal men from Rolls-Royce. They had a lot to do; except for the stock Ford V8 power train (chosen for its relative lightness and a 70% discount from Henry himself), nearly every part had to be custom-designed, and precisely fabricated by hand. Bucky wanted the car to be well finished. He knew that good workmanship would impress onlookers and the media, adding to a convincing demonstration of his ideas.

There was only one major problem left to solve. The car was extraordinarily stable in still air, but even Bucky described driving the Dymaxion in gusty conditions as an endless, nerve-wracking crosswind landing in a small airplane. The aircraft cable-and-pulley steering was thought to be at fault. An airplane's course needn't be correct to the fraction of an inch, but a car's does. The loose feel made the unfamiliar rear steering even trickier to master. Thicker cables and five different rear wheel swivel geometries were tried, but the car remained unacceptably twitchy.

The amazing maneuverability also caused some problems: a vigorous twist of the steering wheel could swing the tail way out beyond the front wheels' tracks,

Fig. 4-6

The original drawing of the Dymaxion logo.

threatening to swat anything in its path. A violent swerve might tear the rear tire from the rim. Test drivers could not get used to it; they rumbled the tail against guard rails more than once. Bucky himself overturned in an encounter with an embankment, injuring his wife and daughter.

As he so often recommended, Bucky "reformed the environment instead of the man" by installing steering restrictors that kept the tail's path safely inside that of the front wheels at road speeds. Centering springs made the straight-ahead position easier to feel. All that helped, but adroit moves still required practice and caution.

Today, an ergonomics expert would be retained to solve such problems, but ergonomics—which studies the operator-machine interface—was not a discipline in 1933. There were no guiding principles to follow. Intuition doesn't always provide marketable answers especially when time is short. The design of proper steering would need more time.

Other problems were social. Creditors pounded on the door. Bucky's family repeatedly wrote to ask when they'd see him again. And there was a mystery: as the deadline approached, work slowed. It took Bucky a while to realize why: His employees knew that they'd be unemployed when the car was finished. To keep them working on the first car, he started work on a second that he hoped potential investors would buy.

The crew met the deadline, and the first car rolled out the Bridgeport, CT, factory door to astound a crowd of local citizens and a well-chosen group of prominent people. (Bucky was very much aware of the power of publicity.)

Coming from a heritage of aircraft and boat building, a plywood and bentwood framing supported the aluminum body of the first complete car. The brochure claimed a road-ready weight of 1850 pounds (839.2 kg)— not much heavier than a VW Beetle, yet 6 feet (1.8 meters) longer. The huge, perforated rear suspension "A-frame" hinged on the front axle, ensuring that all wheels stayed perpendicular to the road at all times. Road grip and ride were exceptional: The car could be driven fast across a plowed field without disturbing the passengers, and it bettered a local stock car track record—with a full load of race promoters aboard!

The silver Dymaxion (Figs. 4-9 through 4-11) caused a sensation that no automobile could engender today. A drive up New York's Park Avenue gridlocked a significant portion of midtown Manhattan. Excluded from the annual auto show at Madison Square Garden, Bucky parked his car near the street entrance, effectively upstaging Detroit's finest anyway, and causing a notorious daily traffic snarl. The car was mobbed everywhere it went. The press hailed the car as a major force that would help end the Depression.

Media accolades quickly turned to sneers when a politician's car rammed and overturned the Dymaxion near the entrance to the Chicago Fair, killing its famous race driver (the canvas top caved in on him), and seriously injuring two influential passengers—would-be investors about to depart on the Graf

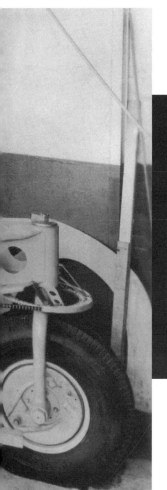

Raising the "bustle" of the second car exposes the steering arrangement. The single wheel could be turned to 90 degrees, giving extraordinary maneuverability. Limiters prevented excessive steering angles at speeds above 15 mph (25 kph). The partially restored car (it's car #2) is on display at the National Automobile Museum in Reno, NV. Among the classic cars its own age, it looks like a cross between a spaceship and a pollywog come to the wrong party.

Fig. 4-8

Fig. 4-7

Zeppelin. Bucky was not allowed to examine the wreck for a month. The politician's involvement was not acknowledged until the coroner's inquest, which exonerated the Dymaxion's design. Of course, newspapers didn't report that.

After the moderately damaged car was repaired (and the roof strengthened), Gulf Oil used it in a campaign to publicize aviation gasoline. Bucky's friends encouraged him to finish the second complete car for the 1934 Chicago Fair in order to regain the Dymaxion's reputation as the design of the future. While it was being built, the flamboyant symphony orchestra conductor, Leopold Stokowski ordered a fancier, heavier Dymaxion for his wife. There wasn't the time or money to develop either car as the definitive pre-production prototype.

Fig. 4-9

The slippery 1933 Dymaxion could go 120 mph (193 kmh), got 30 miles per gallon (7.8 L/100 km), and could carry 11 passengers. The belly was sleek too; even the suspension was enclosed. The shape was aerodynamically correct for the "jet-stilt" levitator Bucky intended it to be someday, but not ideal for an automobile: wind-wander at high speeds was a serious problem.

Carefully chosen nose contours maintained a partial vacuum in front of the first car, greatly improving performance. Cabin ventilation entering around the headlight could be "air conditioned" with a block of dry ice in the duct. When the curved plastic windshield refused to shed water and snow as predicted from aircraft experience, it was replaced by small safety-glass facets (with unsatisfactory wipers). Crushable balsa wood blocks inside the nose gave a measure of protection to front seat passengers in the event of a head-on collision. A small skylight let the driver check the rooftop rearview mirror.

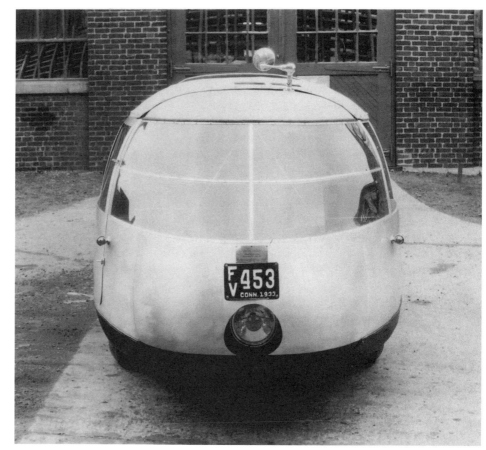

Fig. 4-10

Bucky with the first complete car. Rear-wheel steering made one-pass parallel parking easy—just nose into the space and whip in the tail. (Bucky didn't mention that *leaving* the parking space required awkward backing out into traffic.) The car could pivot around a front wheel, U-turning in its own length at speeds up to 15 mph! A faster U-turn would tear the tire off the rim. Note the huge backup lamp that steered with the wheel.

Fig. 4-11

The handmade body panels of the second car take shape. According to automaker Walter Chrysler, developing the Dymaxions would have cost his company three times more time and four times more money than Fuller expended. Bucky insisted that individuals and small teams can always work more efficiently than any large company.

Fig. 4-12

The yachty interior of the first car could be equipped to seat 11 passengers, truck 3/4-ton of cargo, or fold into a queen-size bed—all without affecting weight distribution. Oversize doorsills covered the arms of the enormous rear suspension A-frame seen in Fig 4-7. Modifications made the second and third cars roomier, but they still had an annoyingly high floor, necessary to clear the articulated chassis.

Fig. 4-13

This crude rig of jacks and scales measured the second Dymaxion's wheel loadings, and verified its excellent resistance to overturning (except when skidding sideways). Louvers directed expanded hot radiator and engine air into the low-pressure wake, reducing drag.

Fig. 4-14

Fig. 4-15

Separated at birth. The 1933 Dymaxion used the same engine and drive train as the Ford of the same year next to it, but was much faster and more fuel-efficient. Bucky acidly pointed out that the Ford would actually have less air resistance if it drove tail first! The Dymaxion's shockingly different design caused massive traffic tie-ups. It represented a new definition of the word "car." Roof bump is rearview periscope.

Fig. 4-16 Top view of car 2.

Built for symphony orchestra conductor Leopold Stokowski, the third car impressed the crowds at the 1934 Chicago World's Fair. Bodywork by Waterhouse (the firm that made bodies for heavy Packard luxury cars) and a Formica® interior brought the weight to an unflyable 3000 pounds (1360 kg). The new tailfin failed to quell wind-wander. This car was reportedly scrapped after 300,000 miles (482,790 km), but stories of its existence continue. Perhaps Elvis has it.

Fig. 4-17

With the last of his investor's money, and his own inheritance, Bucky finished the second and third cars. By then, Bucky knew that it would be best to steer the front wheels, with the rear wheel swivelling only for tight situations. Unfortunately, no stock front-wheel-drive car with suitable parts existed, and Bucky couldn't raise the money to develop his own. Tight finances also prevented the use of the automatic transmission and disc brakes he had been considering. The new cars did get yet another all-new chassis to improve the ride and handling.

Stokowski's emerald-green machine was a big hit at the Chicago Fair, but Bucky couldn't afford to produce one for Amelia Earhart, or the three ordered by the Russian embassy. The fatal crash had frightened away all the investors, including those interested in selling a Dymaxion car with a Curtis-Wright aircraft engine as the top-line Studebaker.

To pay his debts, Bucky gave the second car to the men who had made it, sold the factory and its tools, and laid off his talented team. The experience convinced him that renting a shop and machine tools was the best strategy. It was the last time he tied up exploration money in his own prototyping facilities. He didn't stop thinking about Dymaxion Transport, though. He still had to make the perfected third prototype.

The Little Car That Wasn't

In 1943, Bucky proposed a radical car for industrialist Henry Kaiser, who, like Preston Tucker, thought that the end of World War II would be a good time to challenge Detroit's stagnated, inefficient designs. Bucky's new four-passenger Dymaxion design was light, roomy, aerodynamic, fuel-efficient, and well-matched to the needs of most people. Much smaller than his first cars, it was in effect the third prototype—the one that utilizes the lessons of the first two to arrive at a refined version, with all major problems solved.

Light weight is a major means of doing more with less. Bucky understood that lightness brings more lightness as well as better fuel economy. A lightweight body doesn't need a heavy, powerful engine in order to perform well. A lighter engine makes the car lighter still. Brakes, wheels, tires, and suspension can all be lighter. There's no need for power brakes or steering—another weight saving. Add a truly aerodynamic body, and gasoline mileage soars with no penalty in utility or driving satisfaction.

Unfortunately, the proposed car was so advanced that an affordable, road-testable prototype could not be constructed from existing mechanical parts as had

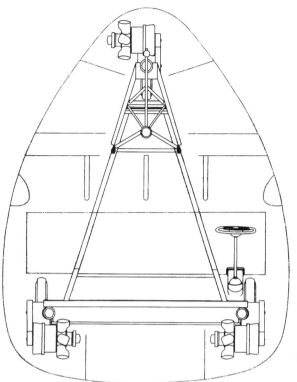

The 1943 Kaiser proposal shows four-abreast seating with luggage space behind, and a 15-horsepower, 5-cylinder radial two-stroke engine at each wheel. Only the rear engine was used for level-highway cruising. Experience has shown that this car would be too wide for today's city traffic. The width would also add unnecessary frontal area which would reduce fuel economy.

Fig. 4-18

been done with the earlier Dymaxion cars. Also, like all three-wheelers, it was not adaptable to the hatchback and tailgated "ranch wagon" body styles that were gaining popularity with returned World War II veterans starting new families. Kaiser rejected it as too radical, and too expensive to develop.

Instead of retreating, Bucky tried again in 1950 with a car that was even more radical (Fig. 4-21). Cars would have to be efficient someday, why not make one that was state-of-the-art? But he'd gone too far. Obsoleting every other car on the road was much more than competitive attack. Bucky didn't realize until years later that banks subtly, but inexorably, deter any truly new auto design that would lower the market value of cars for which they hold the lien. Dealers and banks would be stuck with lots full of unsold old-mode cars. Trade-ins would be worth less, making new cars harder to buy. Tucker encountered the same obstacle at about the same time, with similar results: He lost. So did Bucky.

As with the earlier Kaiser proposal, Bucky's little Dymaxion never progressed beyond drawings. Kaiser eventually produced the Henry J., a cheap, nondescript little car of little merit. Sales were nondescript, too. What would cars be like today if Kaiser had accepted that Dymaxion design?

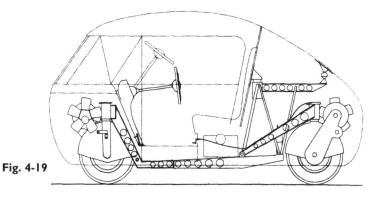

Fig. 4-19

Only 9 feet (2.74 meters) long, the roomy Kaiser takes up little urban road space. The complex chassis of the early Dymaxions has been replaced by a hydropneumatic suspension similar to that used by French Citroën automobiles. It offers a low floor, ultra-smooth ride, and adjustable ground clearance that can be doubled for superior off-road performance as an ultra-stable "3 x 3".

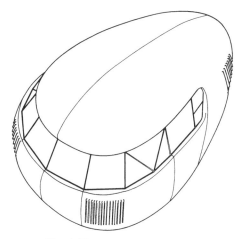

Fig. 4-20

Inspired by studying the cross-current-resistant shape of horseshoe crabs, the aerodynamic form gives minimum drag without crosswind jitters. Only the front wheels steer at road speeds. All three steer for urban agility, permitting sideways crabbing in and out of parking spaces. It could have U-turned inside a standard garage!

Bucky's 1950 design for the Kaiser "Henry J." replaced the earlier piston engines with tiny gas turbines driving paired, skinny tires with low rolling resistance and puddle-slicing resistance to aquaplaning. (Modern tire technology would make duals unnecessary.) A telescopic boom for the rear wheel extends the wheelbase for high speed stability. Henry Kaiser rejected the design as too radical.

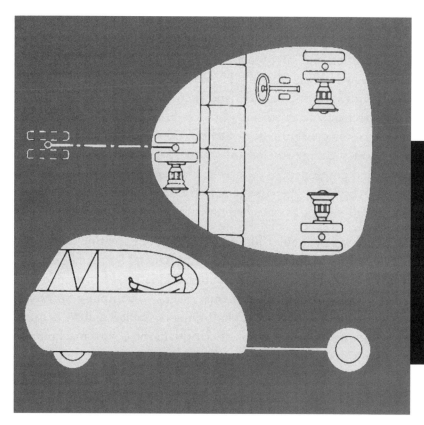

Fig. 4-21

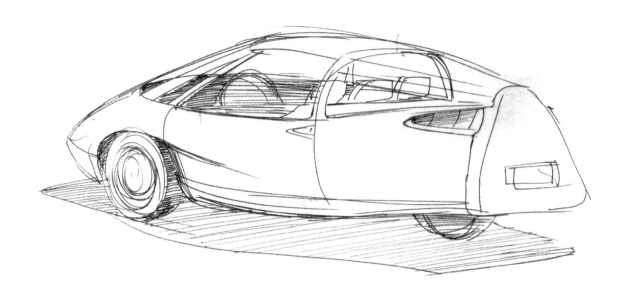

A Dymaxion Hypercar

Bucky's Kaiser car might be more acceptable now. Though it didn't directly address modern pollution and safety requirements, it had many of the basic characteristics of the light, ultra-efficient "Hypercars" first proposed in 1994 by the Rocky Mountain Institute's cofounder and energy expert, Amory Lovins. The Hypercar synergetically takes advantage of a hybrid drive—a system that uses a small, fuel-burning generator set or fuel cell to power an electric motor in each wheel. A modest energy-storage unit (battery, capacitor, or flywheel) furnishes the bursts of power needed for acceleration and hill-climbing, and recovers energy from braking. The arrangement is much lighter, more efficient, and cleaner than an all-electric car weighed down by a ton of batteries.

The Hypercar would weigh about 1000 pounds (453.6 kg), within a few pounds of Bucky's calculation for the proposed 1950 Kaiser. Like the Hypercar, Bucky's could have been made from fiber-reinforced plastic—a "net-shape" material molded into a few large components, exactly to contour with no waste. With one less wheel's worth of weight, rolling resistance, and air drag, a Dymaxion Hypercar might be even more efficient than the Lovins machine. After all (as Bucky insisted), three wheels is all you need.

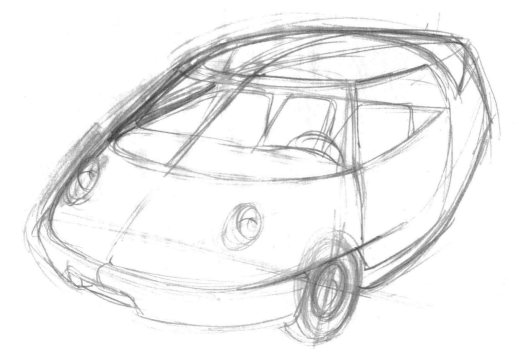

Fig. 4-22

Auto designer Robert Cumberford
sketched this proposal of a Dymaxion
Hypercar to meet today's conditions and
regulations. With only three wheels, it
would be lighter and have less air and
rolling resistance than the astonishingly
logical Hypercars being proposed by
Amory Lovins and his colleagues at the
Rocky Mountain Institute. Vulnerability to
opportunistic lawsuits may be the major
deterrent to Hypercars; accident or injury from any cause whatever would be
blamed on the design, its manufacturer,
and the designer, whether or not the
car was at fault.

THE TRAVELING CARTRIDGE

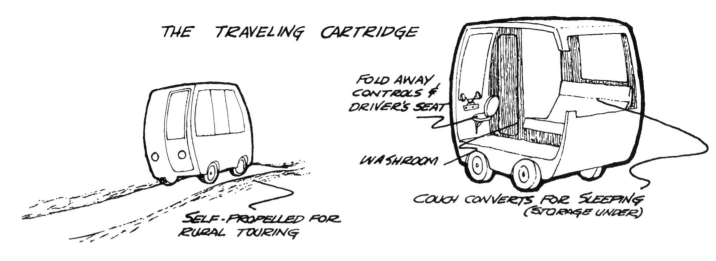

FOLD AWAY CONTROLS & DRIVER'S SEAT

WASHROOM

SELF-PROPELLED FOR RURAL TOURING

COUCH CONVERTS FOR SLEEPING (STORAGE UNDER)

OR·USED AS INTRACITY TRANSIT ON ROADBED PROPULSION SYSTEM

Ship Yourself

Bucky didn't give up on aerial Dymaxion Transport, but he came to realize that individual jet-stilt machines would be too noisy, fuel-hungry, polluting, and anarchic. (Think of 50,000 beery Rose Bowl fans simultaneously rising from the parking lots in roaring Dymaxion Transports!) But Bucky also regarded grandiose air terminals and their chaotic ground connections as silly obstructions to efficient travel.

True to form, he thought world-scale, and proposed a completely computerized global transport system. Type in your destination and desired stopovers on the nearest computer terminal. Insert credit card. Then climb aboard a "cartridge"

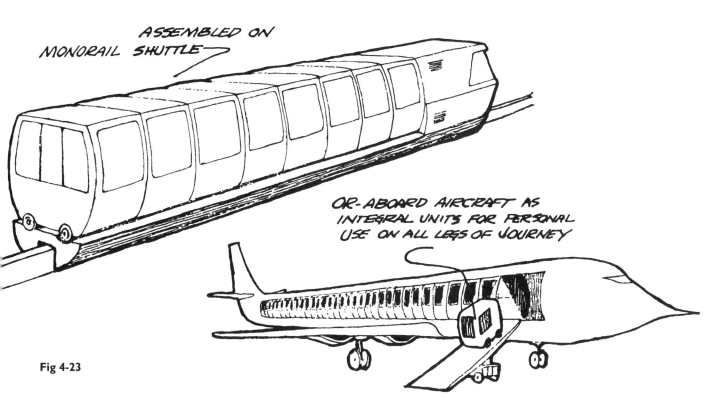

ASSEMBLED ON MONORAIL SHUTTLE

OR-ABOARD AIRCRAFT AS INTEGRAL UNITS FOR PERSONAL USE ON ALL LEGS OF JOURNEY

Fig 4-23

(he likened them to banana slices) at the local station. The system would automatically deliver you anywhere you needed to go by the most expeditious route, complete with all connections and accommodations.

Bucky made futuristic proposals of this sort to get people thinking about existing chaotic, often irrational, arrangements in a more systemic way. The idea might not be feasible at the time, but his images would affect and inspire later thought. How would you design an efficient worldwide transportation system?

Rowing Needles

Few activities can match the exhilarating workout offered by rowing a long, narrow shell known as a "single". Bucky appreciated the intimacy between himself, a simple, human-powered device, and raw nature. It is a satisfying feeling shared by kayakers, bicyclists, and the furiously pedaling pilot of Paul MacCready's extraordinary gossamer aircraft.

Unfortunately, singles are not particularly safe. Twenty-two feet long, but only eighteen inches wide, they are notoriously tippy, and are easily swamped by a minor wave or an inexpert move. Their fragile construction can be fractured merely by positioning a hand or foot in the wrong spot. If a single capsizes or fills in deep water it is virtually impossible to empty and reboard without assistance or going ashore. The situation can be life-threatening in cold water, especially to a solitary rower.

After several close calls, Bucky conceived the Rowing Needles. The catamaran configuration is stable even to a novice. Its sealed hulls "needle" right through waves, while the rower sits above most spray. Climbing aboard does not require skilled balancing, and can be done at sea. Durable materials resist damage, and require little maintenance.

A later prototype of the Rowing Needles had hulls with a better hydrodynamic shape, but they cost far more than the tubular aluminum needles of this first model. It was hard to improve on the original elegant, spare design without adding cost or complexity.

The 1970 patent includes needle sections joined to make a multi-oared racing craft. There's also a needle-hulled sailboat. Bucky attempted to license the patent to a manufacturer, but the deal fell through and he didn't pursue it further. He was doubtless too busy with the major projects of his heyday in the 1970s.

Most observers list the Rowing Needles as "minor innovations," but Bucky once told me that he considered them to be his most refined invention—an exceptionally pure demonstration of his design philosophy.

"Beautiful," he exclaimed, watching a guest rower skim across the peaceful harbor. "Just beautiful."

Fig. 4-24

Though not mathematically geodesic according to Bucky's Synergetic Geometry, Platt Monfort's Geodesic Airolite® boats are close enough. His shockingly light Snowshoe 12® canoe weighs just 13 pounds (5.9 kg), yet can carry a 190-pound (86-kg) paddler.

Fig. 4-25

Fig. 4-26

Beam Me a Pizza

Will a future Sears be able to transmit the goods you ordered? Bucky's graph of increasing travel speeds (Fig. 10-1) implies just that. At a 1966 midnight meeting of friends and colleagues in San Francisco, Bucky said it was important that designers gently introduce the public to the idea of teleportation and the major changes it will bring. If taken by surprise, people might block the technology of ephemeralized transport when it became available.

When asked how teleporting might be done, Bucky replied that energy and information were interchangable, just as energy and matter are interchangable as shown in $E = mc^2$. All systems and structures, right down to molecules and atoms, can be described by frequency and angle. Someday, computers will be able to scan and transmit the full spectrum of such information.

Bucky wasn't sure if life forms could be teleported because the "you" of you is not physical, and thus not scannable. But he assured us that we would live to see objects and materials distributed by some sort of transmission technology.

Bucky was right about the coming capability, and he was right that it would bring big changes. Commercial examples of teleported products are already in use as this is written: Some "record stores" (to use the current anachronism) have a robot computer that can provide a few seconds of music from any available CD. If you choose to buy, your selection is fabricated as you watch, by downloading the digitized music transmitted from the corporate headquarters. Such stores carry no stock, need no employees, and can never run out of items in high demand. The same capability is being applied to videos and books.

It is easy to imagine a store with no stock and no employees becoming an obsolete way of selling. A kiosk would do as well. A home terminal seems inevitable. Does this mean that malls will someday become obsolete as selling devices? Bucky said yes.

The Classic 12® will haul three 200-pound (90.7-kg) people under oars or sail. High-strength materials and innovative construction techniques greatly improve the performance of well-proved hull shapes. Geodesic geometry adds weightless strength. Mr. Monfort's design combines it all to great synergetic advantage.

Chapter 5

Domes

Bucky did not start with the intent to design a dome. When the Wichita Dymaxion Dwelling Machine failed to attract the necessary tooling capital, he turned from money-making business ventures, and went back to where he had started: pure research. He wasn't sure what he would find, but he had confidence that his logic was correct.

A helicopter delivered this lonely geodesic weather and radar dome to the highest crag of Japan's Mt. Fuji. Geodesic domes are often specified for use in extreme conditions where no other structure could survive. Long experience with radar enclosures on the Defense Early Warning (DEW) line across northern Alaska and Canada proved the robustness of the design forty years ago. Because of rapidly changing weather, they had to be installed quickly. Inexperienced Innuit workers could erect a DEW line dome in just fourteen hours under arduous circumstances, but in Washington, DC, a crew of union construction workers took a month to erect an identical dome in mild weather. Bucky's unfamiliar designs often incited interunion squabbling.

Fig. 5-1

Why Domes?

All domes share certain advantages, whether or not they are geodesic. Their compound-curved shape is inherently strong, giving a self-supporting clear span with no columns. Domes are resource and energy-efficient because, of all possible shapes, a sphere contains the most volume with the least surface. This holds true for domal slices of a sphere as well.

A dome has a circular footprint. Of all possible shapes, a circle encloses the most area within the least perimeter. Thus, for a given amount of material, a dome encloses more floor area and interior volume than any other shape.

The minimal surface presents the least area through which to gain or lose heat. Field experience has shown that home-size domes use about one-third less heating fuel than an equally well-insulated conventional home of the same floor area, built of the same materials. (Some domes and conventional homes are better or worse, of course.)

When you double the exterior dimensions of a dome (or any other object), the skin area rises by a factor of four while the volume rises by a factor of eight. This is why supertankers and 747-size aircraft make economic sense: for four times the cost in materials, they can carry eight times the cargo. Larger domes are more efficient because less percent of the contained air is near or touching the skin where most heat loss or gain occurs. Doubling the size of a dome doubles its thermal efficiency.

Bucky suggested that the huge mass of air contained in a big dome would make insulation superfluous, especially if the dome had a double skin. A 100-foot (30.5 meter) diameter hemispherical dome contains about 3.5 (3.2 metric) tons of air. That much mass should not gain or lose heat quickly, but tightly controlled experiments have not yet been done.

The favorable surface-to-volume ratio is not the only reason for a dome's remarkable thermal performance; interior and exterior aerodynamics play a part, too. Architecture libraries have little or no literature on the subject. To my knowledge, no course on architectural aerodynamics is taught anywhere. Except for the calculation of wind loads, most architects do not consider aerodynamics at all. Bucky, however, found aerodynamics to be critical in the design of energy-efficient buildings.

As he discovered in his 4D experiments, a building's heat loss is in direct proportion to its aerodynamic drag (see Fig. 2-5). Unlike most buildings, domes

Elegant dining in The Dome Restaurant in Woods Hole, MA. A daring experiment in 1953, the dome has had its share of problems. It leaked; it was too hot in direct sun; the thin, tightly stretched Mylar® skin proved fragile, and unexpectedly caused the dome to act as a huge, amplifying speaker that annoyed distant neighbors with otherwise modest dinner music. There is no way to test a new dome design without trying it—an expensive proposition that slows development. This dome still exists, reskinned with opaque panels.

Fig. 5-2

Not all geodesic dome restaurants are five-star (except, of course, structurally).

Fig. 5-3

are streamlined. Wind slides smoothly over and around them, generating minimal eddies and vortices to disturb the insulating boundary layer of air that clings to the exterior of any object. (People and animals exposed to conditions of high chill factor instinctively hunch down in a fetal position to reduce their surface area, and to improve their streamlining.) Even three-quarter-spheres like the Montreal dome (Fig. 8-17) have relatively low drag.

A typical rectangular building has high drag. Wind beats directly on the vertical upwind walls and grabs at roof overhangs, removing the heat-holding boundary layer, and creating a high-pressure area. The downwind side is in a turbulent partial vacuum. The turbulence cools the building and the vacuum sucks heated interior air out through cracks around doors, windows, vents, and every other construction flaw on the lee side. The heated air is replaced with cold air sucked in from similar windward gaps. In an older or poorly constructed home, the multiple cracks can add up to an area equivalent to a fully open window!

A dome's heat loss is further reduced by the concave interior. Natural "rolling doughnut" air currents (similar to those seen in a nuclear explosion) prevent stratification; air temperature is nearly the same from floor to apex.

Fig. 5-4a shows the interior air movement when the dome shell is relatively cool, as in winter. Air cooled and made more dense by contact with the walls moves down and across the floor. A heating device located somewhere in the central updraft will distribute heat evenly throughout the dome. Moreover, like an enormous, down-pointing headlight, a dome reflects and concentrates interior radiant heat that would otherwise escape through the skin. The concave interior also bestows a less-expected thermal advantage: self-cooling.

Chilled Domes

In warm weather, the air heated by contact with the relatively warm dome shell naturally circulates as shown in Fig. 5-4b An air conditioning device could be installed in the same location as the heater in Fig 5-4a, but it turns out that air conditioning equipment is not necessary. A dome will cool itself!

Bucky discovered this while building the first Dymaxion Deployment Units. He found that the uninsulated, domelike "tin bins" were satisfyingly cool inside even when the sheet metal skin was literally hot enough to fry an egg. Smoke tests revealed a surprising, counterintuitive fact: heated interior air was being drawn *down* and out under the lower edge of the bin, while cooler air was entering strongly at the top opening. What was going on?

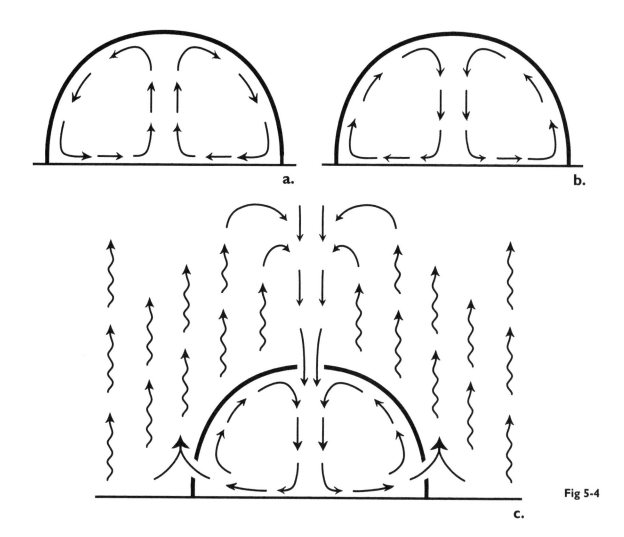

a.

b.

Fig 5-4

c.

Bucky concluded that the white-painted bin and the light-colored area around it were reflecting solar heat, causing an updraft of heated air that slightly lowered atmospheric pressure near the ground. Air inside the dome was being sucked from under the lower edge into the updraft, lowering pressure inside the structure as well (Fig 5-4c).

As hot air rises, it cools. The cooler—and thus denser—air from high above the dome is pulled down through the relatively small opening at the apex of the dome. The small opening acts as a venturi, speeding the flow and dropping the pressure. As the speeding, cooler air enters the interior, it expands suddenly into the dome, further cooling by the Bernoulli effect, a process similar to that inside a refrigerator's cooling coils. Bucky called self-cooling domes "chilling machines."

Fig. 5-5

This uninsulated aluminum dome in Kumasi, Ghana is the first to be deliberately made as a "chilling machine." Natural air currents cause hot air to leave through the hooded openings around the base, drawing cold air in at the top—just as Bucky discovered in his modified grain bin Dymaxion Deployment Units in 1943 (Fig. 2-13). No evaporation pads, refrigeration equipment, or fans are employed. Despite the ferociously hot climate some users of this exhibition dome have complained that it is *too* cool!

Repeated tests performed to the usual scientific standards show that the chilling effect maintains a dome's interior at a temperature about 15% lower than the ambient temperature outdoors, with no fans, compressors, evaporative "swamp coolers," or any other machinery. Controllable vents are the only hardware. The effect works in both dry and humid climates, and occurs whether or not the dome is insulated.

To my knowledge, no tightly controlled tests have been performed to determine the ideal dome proportions and vent arrangements for producing the maximum chilling effect. Such tests would make a worthwhile Ph.D.thesis project. It would be expensive—scale models would not be convincing without scale air—and computer simulations would have to be empirically tested for accuracy at full scale in order to be credible.

As things stand today, there is no peer-reviewed paper proving that the chilling machine effect even exists. But there are domes you can visit, and they remain cool on the hottest days (Fig 5-5). As Bucky liked to say, "Good hardware is irrefutable proof of clear thought."

What Makes a *Geodesic* Dome Special?

The attributes outlined above apply to all except the flattest domes, no matter what their structural system. Geodesic domes have just one major advantage: they are the strongest per pound of material employed. Bucky discovered this by a process that required the mind of a comprehensivist always alert to connections and principles employed by nature.

As the Wichita House progressed toward its unhappy fate, Bucky was perfecting his Dymaxion projection map (Fig. 4-1). His cartographic investigations paid particular attention to the great circle routes used by navigators as the shortest distance—the "geodesic" line—between two points on the globe. It occurred to him that those routes also represented the least possible expenditure of time and energy. Nature always does things in the most economical way, therefore, a network of geodesic lines should provide the geometry for the strongest, most materials-efficient structural system possible. Further investigation revealed that the icosahedron, with its twenty identical equilateral triangles, was probably the key. (See Chapter 3, Synergetics.)

At the same time, Bucky reviewed all the Dymaxion House drawings in his Chronofile, and noticed that the mast always "wanted" to grow in diameter as he stuffed it with more and more functions. It also needed guy wires for stability. In effect, the stabilizing wires or cables defined the true diameter of the mast. Some of the fat-mast structural sketches looked rather geodesic. Why not make the mast fat enough to *be* the building—a building that would need no auxiliary stabilizing?

It didn't take Bucky long to understand that a sphere made up of an icosahedral array of great circle geodesic lines represented the most efficient way to enclose space.

As explained in Chapter 3, a geodesic pattern distributes stress and strain in the most economical way possible. The load is distributed in all directions throughout the entire structure, not just down. The loadbearing efficiency is not constrained by size; geodesic domes actually get stronger as they get larger—a fine example of synergetics at work. (However, as large-radius domes become flatter, they need additional stiffness to prevent dimpling or "punching-in" of vertexes. The Honolulu dome (Fig 5-11) is stiffened by the three-dimensional folding of its sheet metal skin. The Montreal dome (Fig 8-21) achieves the same effect with a three-dimensional arrangement of struts.)

Only minimum-surface, stretched-fabric tension structures can rival a geodesic dome for efficient use of material, but they cannot match its volumetric, strength, durability, and thermal advantages.

Geodesic domes placed in harm's way have withstood the most violent weather on Earth. (Fig. 5-1). Unless ruptured by the ground buckling directly underneath, they are virtually earthquake-proof. Geodesic domes are the strongest, lightest, most resource-efficient shelter available today.

Because geodesic domes are based on optimal synergetic principles—"the coordinates of Universe"—Bucky expected that no more efficient building system would ever be found. He did suggest that the manipulation of force fields might eventually eliminate the need for physical buildings altogether, but he didn't say how this might be done.

A number of critics have contended that Bucky did not invent the geodesic dome. The first one recorded was built in 1922, by Walter Bauersfeld. It served as the framework for a concrete Zeiss planetarium in Jena, Germany. Herr Bauersfeld apparently did not realize what he had; his project description gives no sign that he recognized the synergetic principles represented in his frame design. Though his planetarium projected the heavens on the icosahedron's triangles, he did not attempt to open the icosahedron into a flat map as Bucky later did. He did not use geodesics again, nor did he seek a patent.

Bucky's archives hint that he knew of the Jena dome (it's hard to imagine that he was not aware of it), but his first geodesic models were not copies. They were the first of a long series of investigations into geodesic patterning, dome-making methods, and structural details that he would continue until his death. He patented a number of them. (All his dome patents have expired.)

Fig. 5-6

Bucky's first commercial geodesic dome was this 93-foot (28.3-meter) dome over the court-yard of the Ford Rotunda building in Dearborn, MI. The Rotunda had been Ford's temporary exhibit hall for a fair. When the fair closed, the dome was moved to Dearborn, MI, and rebuilt. Bucky's 8.5-(7.7-) ton dome was the only design the relatively flimsy Rotunda could support. The lightest steel dome would have weighed 160 (144) tons. A *Life* magazine story on the project brought both Bucky and Ford a reputation for advanced engineering, and attracted many students to Bucky's courses.

There can be little doubt that Bucky was the first to discover and develop the only new type of structure in 2000 years. Today, about 200,000 geodesic domes (not counting geodesic playground jungle gyms) enclose far more space than the work of any other architect.

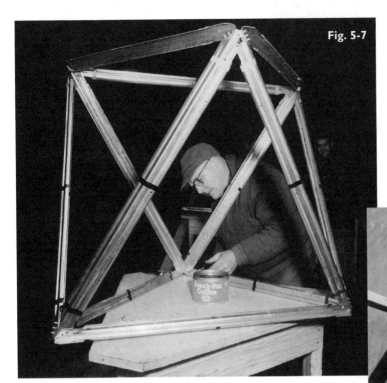

Fig. 5-7

The Rotunda dome was built from 20,960, 5-ounce (142-g) struts riveted into triangles. The triangles were then riveted into 4-pound (1.8-kg) octahedra in six mini-"factories" strategically located around the rim of the Rotunda's roof. This dome was the first architecture ever built to aircraft tolerances. The thousands of jig-drilled holes lined up perfectly.

Fig. 5-8

A burley worker shows that he can carry 2 triangular octet truss "Rafts," each made up of 25 octahedra. Light components reduced the chance of accidents and injury. Clumsy, dangerous construction cranes were not required.

Two workers join raft assemblies around the bottom edge of the growing dome. Only one rivet diameter and one bolt diameter were employed, saving money and reducing the chance of mistakes. Assembly took just 42 days, surprising skeptical Ford engineers.

Fig. 5-9

Fig. 5-10

Workers pose while skinning the large triangle assemblies with the thin, translucent fiberglass panels seen at the far right. The sealing detail proved leaky—not surprising in what amounted to an untested prototype made from unusual materials by workers who had never seen anything like it. (Nobody had.) Attempts to remedy the leaks led to a roofing tar fire that destroyed both dome and Rotunda. They were never rebuilt.

Growing Pains

Yes, there are disadvantages to any dome, whether geodesic or not. Some are without remedy. Domes do not fit certain lot shapes, for instance, especially in dense downtown areas where highrises make the best economic sense. To answer this justifiable complaint, Bucky proposed megastructures and domes with multistory interiors (See Chapter 9).

Domes do not gracefully accept additions. A conceptually simple, attached garage can be an awkward challenge. Appendages such as porches and dormers interfere with a dome's aerodynamics, defile the pure shape, and are apt to leak. If more room is needed and the lot is big enough, it is usually easier to build a separate dome nearby, or "kiss" several together. The interface between touching domes requires careful design, especially when connecting the angles and facets of a geodesic (Fig 2-18). Another possibility: use Chuck Hoberman's articulated geodesics to make a dome that can grow in the manner of a turtle shell (Fig 7-11).

Domes cannot be enlarged by adding a second story but larger, more spherical designs can have one or more decks added inside to take advantage of the volume. Indeed, this is one of the best ways of partitioning a dome. A few geodesic domes have been designed to be raised enough to add a story's worth of triangles or a ring wall at the bottom at a later time.

Some people think that geodesic domes all look the same. The peas-in-a-pod argument has been answered in Chapter 2. The illustrations in this book show that geodesics can take many forms. Indoors, especially in transparent domes, the space gives most people a feeling of rightness. (This claim is corroborated by a tape deck left in a state fair transparent dome for a week, recording the remarks of more than 30,000 people.) The positive feeling may be because geodesic domes based on the icosahedron—as Bucky's are—always involve pentagons. Pentagons abound in examples of the "Divine Proportion" or "Golden Mean" relationships often seen in nature and the work of ancient architects. For centuries, humans have instinctively found that proportion to be particularly agreeable.

Other disadvantages are perversely inherent in the advantages: The rounded, convex interior shape that bestows such desirable thermal properties can cause annoying echoes, though careful design can provide the superior acoustics of a good auditorium (Fig. 5-12). Acoustic *privacy*, however, is poor even when cured of echo effects. Every sound can be heard clearly, anywhere in a dome.

Everyone aboard can hear the proverbial pin drop. Soundproof partitions can help, but they tend to interrupt the dome's natural air circulation patterns.

Those thermally wonderful air patterns also bring some problems. They quickly and evenly distribute smells as well as heat and cool air throughout the dome. Kitchen and bathroom vents must work well to avoid embarassment. More seriously, the natural airflow can distribute fire and smoke with fatal rapidity, making fire-resistant furnishings, escape routes from decks and balconies, and fast-acting automatic extinguishing systems important design considerations. On the other hand, the convex *exterior* shape is ideal for diffusing the radiant heat threat of a nearby fire, and there are no soffit vents or gutters to catch sparks.

The rounded interiors may be efficient, but they are not easily divided in familiar ways. Store-bought furniture, partitions, shelving, cupboards, and appliances are intended for a rectangular layout. They are likely to be an uneasy fit in a dome. Elegant, integrated interiors need expensive custom design work and unusually skilled builders. A mass-produced dome system that included interior furnishings would help to lower costs, but would also restrict choices. It would be a shame to afflict such a useful space with traditional limitations.

Imagination and willingness to explore new ideas for interiors is the best answer. Centuries of traditional interiors have numbed us to the possibilities. We've been trained to accept choices from a limited menu of styles without question. Chapters 2 and 8 discuss some interesting alternatives.

Leaks

'Domes leak' is usually the first complaint heard from people who don't like geodesic domes. The reputation is deserved. It cannot be denied that many geodesic domes have leaked, and that many still leak. Bucky answered the whines and curses of damp domers by retorting, "You wouldn't build a boat full of holes and expect it not to leak, would you?" He also was heard to mutter something about leaky domes being evidence of leaky minds.

Careless and inept builders—there were many among the "counterculture" builders of the 60s and 70s—deserved that comment. They worried him. To prevent gratuitous, inexpert dome building, he had refrained from publishing do-it-yourself instructions. But geodesic "Sun Dome" greenhouse plans sold by *Popular Science* magazine in the 60s, and Lloyd Kahn's *Domebook One* and *Domebook Two* (Pacific Domes 1970-1971) brought the necessary geometry to

These workers in Honolulu, HI, are building a 145 foot (44 meter) Kaiser Aluminum dome from the top down, pulling it up a temporary mast as parts are added to the rim, just as Bucky had done with the Dymaxion Deployment Unit a decade earlier. At other locations, similar domes were supported by a huge balloon that was slowly inflated as parts were added around the bottom. Stamped sheet metal panels and cross braces form shallow tetrahedrons that synergetically act together as a stiff, light, structural skin. No frame is necessary. Temcor® still makes these (and other designs) in many sizes. They've sold more than 4000 of them, making them the world's premier dome makers. They intend to keep that position: A 900 foot (274 meter) dome has been engineered. If erected, it would be the largest clear-span structure ever made.

Fig 5-11

everyone. Domes of many sorts suddenly appeared all over the world, bringing new meaning to the cliché, "Like toadstools after a rain." A few were astonishingly beautiful. Most were not. Nearly all leaked.

Experience had taught Bucky that new ideas are more readily accepted by the general public when presented free of trivial flaws that deflect attention from

Fig 5-12

Just twenty-two hours after workers opened the crates of dome parts flown in from California, this audience listened to a performance by the Hawaiian Symphony Orchestra. The faceted interior did a good job of controlling distracting echo effects.

important advantages and potential. Bucky applauded the evidence of his maxim, "Evolution makes many starts," but he thought the imaginative, often crude domes made by unskilled amateurs would give geodesic domes a bad name. He was right.

But geodesic domes done by meticulous carpenters and professional engineers also leaked. Bucky's first commercial dome, the one over the Ford Rotunda's courtyard (Fig.5-6), burned while workers were making yet another attempt to seal leaks in its fiberglass skin. The otherwise magnificent dome at Montreal dripped enough to flood the main floor ankle deep. Bucky and Anne never did manage to seal their own plywood dome-home while at Southern Illinois

University—most embarrassing! It became obvious that building a permanently tight dome was not a trivial matter, but it took years to understand why. More years went by before successful, long-lived sealing was finally achieved.

A new technology may have an entirely new *type* of problem that takes engineers and trades workers by surprise. The tendency of geodesic domes to leak is an example of such a problem. Geodesic expansion and contraction is the culprit. As discussed in Chapter 3, the geodesic pattern distributes stress—the forces acting on the structure—evenly and almost instantly throughout the entire dome. That's what gives geodesic domes their remarkable strength per pound of material. Strain—the structural deformation caused by stress—is also distributed over the entire structure, but not necessarily evenly.

When the sun heats one side of a dome, the warmed materials expand, locally enlarging the diameter of the dome by a small, but significant amount. Expansion effects can also occur over the entire dome surface if the interior is a markedly different temperature than the exterior. Material expansion is an inexorable force; think of how easily expanding ice breaks a steel water pipe. When expansion stress and strain reach unexpanded materials, the asymmetrically loaded geodesic structure tries to distribute that load evenly. Something has to give.

A dome consisting of separate panels may open gaps between the panels. In other locations, it may tighten the gaps, squeezing out seals or caulk. In a dome with a one-piece skin—welded metal or fiberglass, for instance—the dome distributes the strain by distorting. On a hot sunny day, a subtle bulge may even be visible to the naked eye. The bulge moves as the sun angle changes.

Any distortion or panel movement can open cracks around doors, windows, vents, dormers, and other non-geodesic features. Repeated hot-cold cycles can break the grip of sealants and fasteners. Rubber gaskets around glazing may act as linear water pumps. Thermal cycling can also cause fatigue cracks—with consequent leaks—in the material itself.

No available caulk—not even the permanently gooey marine grades—can withstand this for long unless joints have been specifically designed to take punishment. No crack-covering tape or mastic will last, nor will most sprayed-on foam—especially when exposed to sunlight. It is common to see handmade domes disfigured by repeated attempts to seal between panels, each remedy messier than the one before, layer upon layer until the unfortunate structures resemble the droppings of some giant, prehistoric beast. Most frustrated (maddened is perhaps more accurate) owners of wooden domes eventually resort to tarpaper and shingles, another temporary solution. A number of domes have been abandoned or demolished as hopeless.

There is a reason for all those roofing contractors listed in the Yellow Pages: The roofs of nearly all conventional buildings leak sooner or later. Domes are mostly roof. Inexpertly designed domes leak sooner rather than later, because the expansion and contraction effects hasten the degradation of traditional roofing materials that are not notably durable to begin with. Worse, many familiar techniques and materials are not well-suited to the geometry of domes. A typical contractor has little experience with folding tarpaper, and trimming or bending shingles into odd shapes. Leaks are common at the tricky points where many triangles meet. The nearly horizontal shingles at the top of a dome may scoop horizontal rain instead of shedding it, and they can be violently ripped away by the "backing-a-chicken-into-the-wind" effect.

It need not be that way. Dome builders have learned a few things since Bucky's first one forty-seven years ago. Even designs that use common building materials and procedures are acceptably tight these days, though they are still subject to all of the problems that Bucky sought to avoid with his industrially produced Dymaxion Houses.

Today's best commercial designs not only don't leak, they *can't* leak. Their permanent, precision parts are mass-produced in automated factories, giving a very high standard of fit and finish not vulnerable to careless assembly at the building site. Clever, long-lasting silicone seals keep working without fatigue. Some designs don't even require seals. These well-engineered domes best represent what Bucky always had in mind. They are pure synergetics made visible.

Chapter 6

The Sorcerer's Apprentices

The first big geodesic dome, a 50-foot (15.24-meter) design, easily supports its construction crew as it goes up near Montreal in 1950. The stubby tubular "sprits" carry a pattern of tension wires that add stiffness (and interesting wind-hum). A fabric skin was stretched tightly under the frame. Calculations and construction were led by Don Richter and Jeffrey Lindsay, ex-Fuller students from the Chicago Institute of Design. This dome has been moved many times.

I do not engage in class instruction with repetitive curricula. — RBF

"Mind wind" is what Bucky called the feeling of imminentness when an idea is in the air. As soon as he realized the synergetic attributes of geodesics, mind wind became a typhoon of possible dome designs and applications, far more than he could ever explore as an individual through his own companies, Fuller Research Foundation and Geodesics, Inc. It seemed unlikely that venture capitalists, existing corporations, or the government would pay for exploratory research on an unproven idea with unknown market value. How could he speed geodesic evolution?

The answer was to recruit college students. Most were from architecture and design departments. Fortunately, Bucky had enough experience and prestige (and notoriety) to hold classes and research seminars at progressive schools, despite his lacking a degree. He didn't have any problem filling his classes; truly new, nonestablishment ideas have always attracted idealistic students. Unless suppressed, young people intuitively urge the next stage of evolution.

The arrangement was good for all concerned. The schools could point to a prestigious visiting professor, students received academic credit, and Bucky got something much more valuable than the welcome stipend: As his many-minded student teams investigated every nuance and blind alley, many of his ideas were quickly taken to the proof-of-concept stage. By bringing his

Fig 6-1

laboratory to the classroom, he didn't have to buy materials, hire help, or rent facilities. It was also an irresistable opportunity to subversively augment his students' overspecialized education with a bit of training in comprehensive thought.

Bucky rarely engaged his students in simulations, and never in contrived excercises. He gave them total responsibility for the task, but no hints as to how it might be done. Classwork consisted of real experiments being done for the first time. He often gave different schools identical assignments, deliberately concealing the existence of the groups from one another. The duplicate work ensured that evolution would indeed make many starts—one of his favorite subjects—and provided the assurance that comes from replicated experiments.

The policy also prevented cross-fertilization and mutual assistance. Some students were miffed by learning later that the findings of another team would have prevented them from needlessly working to a known dead-end. Despite protests (including mine), Bucky insisted that reinventing and rethinking was best. Maybe it was; he and his hardworking apprentices could point to an astonishing list of ideas refined into practice. I've wondered lately how he'd handle the worldwide Internet connections of a roomfull of today's apprentices.

Complaints did not extend to doing true research. The experiments were in dynamic, thrilling contrast to library research, which consists mostly of looking up what someone else has already done. (In this sense, a surprising pecent of college courses amount to a history of their discipline.) With a week or two of hard work, an enthusiastic class could—and usually did—travel the path from speculation, to research, to drawings, and, in most cases, to models or full-scale demonstrations.

Destructive win/lose competition gave way to cooperation. Participants divided tasks and responsibilities. Goaded by Bucky's boundless energy (didn't he *ever* sleep?), they often worked twenty-four-hour shifts. The blazing pace added to an ambience of discovery and excitement that kept the project boiling. Problems were solved as fast as they appeared, sometimes by new teams assembled for the purpose. Students had to think things through comprehensively—often for the first time in their lives. There was a strong incentive to be daringly right. They often were.

The results were visible, touchable, sometimes spectacular physical entities, not mere studies culminating in speculative suggestions. The most gratifying result was that the photographs impressed your family at Christmas. Without pictures, the work would have been hard to explain to grandma.

Fig. 6-2

Bucky's first attempt at a large dome was this 48-foot (14.6-meter) "flopahedron" at Black Mountain College in 1949. Made of metal venetian blind slatting, it was too flexible to stand. Some unverified accounts claim that the dome was reinforced and finally erected, but the ribbony chaos of this photograph makes that seem unlikely, and there is no photographic evidence of success to be found (so far) in the Chronofile.

A more probable explanation is that Bucky built this first prototype deliberately weak, a tactic he learned from Henry Ford. Strengthening the points of failure just enough to work satisfactorily assures optimized materials efficiency. Though crude compared to computer simulations, the method works surprisingly well; Bucky's next dome (Fig. 8-1) was satisfyingly strong. (The strength of Ford's Model T—the first product to be designed using this method— was legendary. Bucky thought highly of Ford's design strategies and worldwide logistics.)

The experience of working with Bucky was both exciting and scary—more of an adventure than a class. It was a great way to learn. It adorned your portfolio with a record of unique, dirty-hands, design-science pioneering, far ahead of the usual student work. For several of Bucky's students, it was the beginning of a career of applied geodesics: Don Richter, for instance, founded Temcor, the company that built the 164-foot (50-meter) dome over the South Pole and the 415-foot (126.5-meter) dome in Long Beach, CA intended for Howard Hughes' enormous Spruce Goose seaplane. Kenneth Snelson made the first tensegrity construction, and later became famous for his tensegrity sculpture.

For Snelson and several others, working with Bucky was not always a pleasant experience. Their work and Bucky's became inextricably entangled, and it was difficult to determine clearly whose ideas were whose. Arguments over credit were inevitable as students and other investigators enlarged upon Bucky's discoveries. Bucky would say, "I built that dome," when in fact his students had built it. In those days, it was expected that a professor would refer to student work in that way (many still do). Moreover, if it hadn't been for his discoveries, the students would have had nothing to work on.

Nevertheless, the affected students were understandably rankled. Others were unable to comprehend the spirit of working without profit as the primary motive. They felt exploited, but because there was no evidence of Bucky getting rich, those complaints subsided. (He never did accumulate riches.)

Bucky gave credit where it was due (including to Snelson), but he often added a laconic, ". . . for his version of my invention." Like many inventors who have faced years of sneers and invisibility, he needed—and demanded—recognition. He didn't always get it. The sparkling dome at Disney's Epcot Center in Florida may be the most famous geodesic dome in the world, but there is no mention of his name anywhere on it. Medard Gabel, director of The World Game Institute (Chapter 10), relates that Bucky was annoyed and disappointed by the lack of credit until it occurred to him that he himself didn't refer to an airliner as a "Wright Brothers Boeing 747."

Bucky also suffered from a phenomenon that afflicts and frustrates designers who illuminate a concept so deeply and well that observers cannot remember what life was like without it. The idea is so logical, and so obviously right that it goes into the public mind instantly and painlessly, totally overrunning the old way of thinking.

Because the previously invisible idea is made so obvious, people will not give credit to the discoverer. To combat this phenomenon, and to deter

Fig. 6-3

This minimum-cost shelter was formed from corrugated cardboard cut and scored (grooved) into strips of triangles by a standard box-making machine. Panels were waterproofed with stinky polyester resin. Shipped as a flat bale, the strips were rapidly stapled together on-site. As with all domes, anchoring against high winds was critical: the first prototype blew away several times (once with me in it). University of Michigan students developed versions for the Marine Corps and a kid's summer camp.

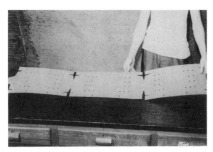

North Carolina State students learned a lot of geometry while patterning the basic component of a cardboard dome. Because complex geodesic structures are especially vulnerable to the consequences of "accumulated error," patterns must be precise even in low-tech cardboard. Custom-fitting the final component of a dome is considered proof of ineptitude.

Fig. 6-4

Fig. 6-5

The thin, floppy cardboard stamping is first folded into triangular tubes to give it stiffness.

A basic triangle takes shape. In mass-production, this could be done by machine. On site, this sort of repetitious work is best done barn-raising style, with many hands directed by a knowledgable, disciplined leader. It's a good idea to assign fussy inspectors, too.

Fig. 6-6

incompentent applications that could give his inventions a bad name, Bucky spent a lot of time and money securing patents. The money he made from them went right back into his research.

Students at Work

North Carolina's astonishing Black Mountain College (long gone, alas) was the scene of the first large-scale experiment performed by Bucky's students. Until then, their work had been confined to indoor models. In 1949, a 48-foot (14.6-meter) dome was fashioned from thin metal venetian blind slatting, which turned out to be too flexible to support a hemisphere of that diameter (Fig. 6-2). Bucky pondered the lessons learned from that experience, then produced a more modest 14-foot (4.26-meter) folding dome—a size that students at Chicago's Institute of Design had already proved feasible. It worked

The basic triangular pieces are bound together with fiberglass filament tape to form hexagonal or pentagonal "rafts" that simplify the final assembly of the dome. The small, light-colored guide model at left center on the floor inside the dome reduces frustrating (and embarrassing) assembly errors. Not many women took Bucky's courses, but there were usually a few who enthusiastically joined the teams.

Fig. 6-7

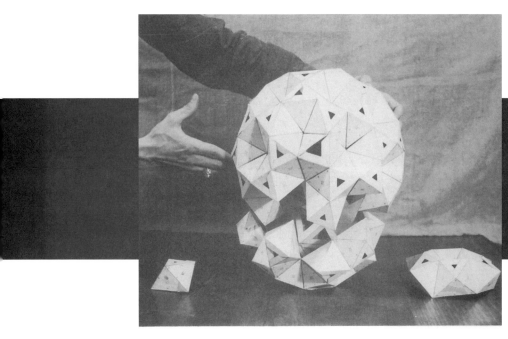

It's all octahedra. This octasphere is the sort of experiment that can reveal unsuspected relationships that are hard to visualize.

Fig. 6-8

University of Minnesota students designed and built the tooling, then produced the fiberglass tubular compression struts for this tensegrity dome.

Bucky usually asked students to organize into teams, each with a specific task. Teams then divided the work among their members. Individual responsibility and a common goal soon developed noncompetitive cooperation that greatly speeded the project. This team finds out first hand how messy resin can be as they lay up the fiberglass struts. (Today, they'd wear masks and goggles.)

Fig. 6-9

Stacked parts await assembly. The cigar-shape of the strut matches the distribution of the compression load on it—an example of doing more with less. In this information age, we'd call it "replacing material with information." Efficient geometry increases corporate know-how and profits without reducing product quality.

Students usually obtained unusual materials free from manufacturers anxious to find new applications. Bucky taught a useful tactic for that purpose: Always go to the CEO first. Underlings will often refuse requests that might bring a reprimand; a polite "No" is safe. Even if they don't turn you down, they'll kick the request upstairs to the land of endlessly delayed approval. If approached in a spirited, but professional manner, the CEO will most likely order a subordinate to fulfill your request immediately. It's an effective move. Bucky's students literally got truckloads of materials in this way.

Fig. 6-10

Fig 6-11

The tensegrity dome begins to take shape. Note how the struts are loaded only under compression from the ends. They don't touch. Compression members are islands. Of course, the cables can only accept tensile loads. Tension is continuous. The division of duty uses materials in the most efficient way, synergetically adding materials efficiency to the already efficient geodesic geometry. Bucky claimed that Universe consists of "islands of compression in a sea of tension," and expected structures made in that way would prove to be ultimately efficient.

well, demonstrating the remarkable strength and light weight of a practical geodesic structure. The 50-lb (22.8-kg) dome was also the first try at a "Garden-of-Eden" transparent, climate-controlling shell (Fig. 8-1). A similar dome was later used to shelter another student-developed idea—the "Autonomous Package" (Fig. 8-2).

Over the years, students at hundreds of colleges and universities worked on a wide variety of dome geometries and designs—many of them intended to take maximum advantage of specific materials. Bucky focused on the use of materials that were produced in continuous processes with little waste that could not be reprocessed. Cardboard seemed particularly attractive. All it lacked was water, fire, and insect resistance, attributes that could easily be added to the sloppy stew before it was formed into sheets.

There are many ways to make cardboard domes. The simplest is to fold it into great-circle strips of triangles—one pointed up, the next pointed down—that are overlapped and stapled together like giant shingles to shed water. Because such domes have no folded sections framing the panels, they can easily be distorted and "punched-in." The 14-foot (4.26-meter) University of Michigan dome (Fig. 6-3) needed wooden reinforcements to withstand snow loads, and was unusually vulnerable to total blow-away because the stake-down loops pulled through the cardboard in strong winds.

Another cardboard design is shown in Figs. 6-4 through 6-7. After it was assembled, erected, and anchored, the framework was covered with a tight-fitting, plastic "bathing cap" to provide shelter. The same sort of triangular frame members could also be directly folded into the edges of cardboard triangles or diamonds, making a thick-rimmed tray. The most successful cardboard domes were made this way. A 42-foot (12.8-meter) cardboard dome won the grand prize at Italy's Triennale exhibition in 1954.

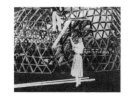

For all their advantages of low cost, paperboard domes had a problem that was simple to fix conceptually, but difficult to vanquish in the field: the material loses its compression strength when it gets wet. (Wet *tensile* strength remains high.) Coating the the material with paint or resin before assembly, or after the dome is completed, is not sufficient. A single pinhole in the coating will let water soak the interior of the board.

Cardboard that has been impregnated with waterproofing is more durable, but is also more expensive, may smell nasty, and can be difficult to recycle. Fire resistance may be compromised by the waterproofing. Students also tried foil-coated board and several types of "bathing cap" covers. Nothing worked reliably. Even when rain wasn't a problem, condensation on the interior was. (An energy-efficient answer to condensation remains to be found.)

Bucky also experimented with FomeCor®. These kraft-paper-clad plastic foam panels are waterproof and strong, but burn enthusiastically, and cost much more than cardboard. Many successful domes have been made from this material. Unfortunately, its cost places it in the difficult limbo of being too expensive to be temporary, and too flimsy to be permanent.

Nevertheless, paperboard and its derivatives and imitators remain a promising possibility. Perhaps Gridcore®, a recent rigid panel made from much the same ingredients as cardboard, will provide the first truly inexpensive, permanent geodesic dome. Perhaps some of Bucky's students' students will make the first one.

Experiments in fiberglass were typical of Bucky's enthusiasm for new materials. World War II had made fiberglass practical, and it was well on the way to taking the place of wood in boats. That had the effect of bringing inexpensive, but very strong recreational boats to the market for the first time. Above all, they were maintenance-free. Owners could spend their time boating instead of repairing rot, and painting the craft yet again. Of course, Bucky thought that those attributes would make fiberglass ideal for buildings. As a "net shape" material it can be formed to almost any shape without waste.

Learn a Lot, Learning Fast

In the summer of 1981, Amy C. Edmondson had been working just ten months in Bucky's office as his engineering assistant. Here, she tells what it was like to find out how Bucky managed to get so much done. Hundreds—maybe thousands—of his ex-students could tell similar tales of learning and teaching at its exciting best. — JB

"We are in a remote ski-resort, a hundred-and-twenty miles from the nearest airport (Reno, Nevada), for a late-summer conference of business people. Bucky is scheduled to lecture for a total of thirty-six hours during the six days, and I am looking forward to listening and learning. Crouched by my balsawood model, I am thrilled (and relieved) by the confirmation of months of agonizing mathematics. It works. Now it's finished and we will celebrate, I think maybe with some ice cream. Bucky thoughtfully inspects my model, nods, and looks up.

"Suddenly, the unexpected. He is not joking; his voice is matter-of-fact: Bucky fully expects the hundred or so conference attendees to construct (led by me) a full-scale prototype of a dome I just finished the calculations for last week. The glue on my model is not yet dry. I begin to suspect that his eighty-six years are catching up with him. 'I know for a fact,' runs the voice inside my head, 'these people are here with felt-tip pens, NOT with bandsaws and drill presses.' I feel sad that Bucky will have to find out the hard way.

"No ice cream yet; he wants me to calculate the weight ("assume Douglas fir") of tomorrow's dome, figure out the stresses ("use good quality wood, not too many knots"), then tell someone what materials we'll need. 'How am I going to tell him?' I wonder, embarrassed, dreading the confrontation.

"New to the job, I hadn't yet seen Bucky Fuller in action; I didn't know that the sight of all these people would evoke irresistable images of past projects, of campuses and students and domes built, it would seem, out of thin air. I didn't know how many "impossible" tasks became sudden joyful history, how many structures were completed overnight, in how many different countries. To Bucky, a captive audience of one-hundred able-bodied Americans appearing right after the completion of his latest geodesic design was an open invitation!

"It turns out, of course, that he knows just what he's doing. He knows that a truck will start towards Reno immediately to buy the necessary lumber; he knows that eager carpenters in the crowd will soon surface and offer their skills. So will contractors, guys with muscles, people with energy, hands, minds. . . The news flies around the complex. History in the making. He knows that his newest development, a prototype, a chance to participate in a tangible accomplishment such as this will tie people together, tantalize, excite, convince. I am the one learning—not the hard way at all—but rapidly, adrenaline flowing, excitement building. I begin to realize that something is really happening here. I soon will find myself thinking it's as if people have been waiting their whole lives to put down their felt-tip pens and stand outside for hours holding two-by-fours in place until their necks ache, with their eyes wide open, listening to urgent instructions flying back and forth. This group will go home exhausted, rejuvenated, awed. None of us will ever forget it.

"Twenty-four hours and eight-hundred dollars later, a twenty-five-foot diameter geodesic dome stands complete, exhibiting a strength unpredicted by the relative frailty of its parts. The deceptively fragile-looking structure is the patient model for hours of photographing, the tolerant scaffold for amazed climbers (Can it really support me?), the makeshift chapel for a wedding (scheduled to take place two weeks later, but moved up in eager celebration of our accomplishment), and finally, an education.

"How many campuses were electrified in this way? I wonder, how many groups have shared this elation? I begin to understand that this sense of urgency, this skilful channeling of human energy, is the secret behind Fuller's eighty-six years of perpetual motion."

Chapter 7

Instant Domes

Bucky explored several ways of efficiently deploying and retrieving domes:

- *They can be specially designed to be erected and taken down easily.*

- *They can be air-lifted to the site complete.*

- *They can unfold from a smaller configuration, like a flower.*

Here's an example of each method. Other chapters have more. Portable shelter is a major feature of Bucky's "One Town World."

Students at Washington University, St. Louis, MO, ready their bundled, air-deliverable, "Flying Seedpod Dome" for quick deployment.

Fig. 7-1

Each ball-jointed vertex is fitted with a pneumatic actuating cylinder charged with air at 200 pounds per square inch. They tighten a cable net that pulls the dome into shape.

Fig. 7-2

A pull on the control lanyard (plus a bit of manual encouragement) erects the 42-foot (12.8-meter) diameter dome in less than a minute. Plans called for a tightly tensioned fabric skin to be hung from the geodesic framework. Earth anchors completed the installation. (Anchors are *always* necessary on any dome) Folding is not as quick and easy, but is still remarkably fast for a structure of this size.

Fig. 7-3

Fig. 7-4

Bucky gleefully watches an aircraft carrier's elevator bring a 36-foot diameter dome to the flight deck. It will be airlifted by helicopter to a new airstrip being established on land. The scheme worked well, though the initial flight must have been harrowing to Bucky and his colleagues—and of course, to the brave pilot who first tried it.

A U.S. Marine Corps helicopter makes off with a 36-foot (11-meter) diameter geodesic dome at 60 knots (111 kmh), fulfilling Bucky's dream of delivering complete structures directly from factory to site. Domes behave very well while being heli-towed, making air delivery a reasonable and economical possibility for instant shelter. Bucky's students developed the first ones to fly.

Fig. 7-5

Uh-oh. Bucky strongly advocated learning by experience, and occasionally, the lesson was a hard one. This foil-coated-cardboard Marine Corps dome reportedly became involved in rotor downwash from the helicopter that was attempting to place it gently on the site. Another account leaves out the helicopter, and asserts that a wind gust caught the dome before it was properly anchored. A third source tells of torrential rain softening the dome into terminal mush. All versions agree that nobody was hurt (at least not physically). When experiments fail, flourishing rumors diffuse blame, permitting the work to continue.

Fig. 7-6

Fig. 7-7

These 100-foot (30.5-meter) international trade fair domes were specially designed for fast (two-day) erection and takedown by unskilled local labor wherever they appeared. Simple design, color-matched parts, and picture-book instructions ensured correct assembly regardless of language or literacy. The fabric skin was pulled into a taut, nonflapping, hyperbolic paraboloid ("hy-par") contour at each hub, giving the solid feel of a permanent structure. As the domed U.S. trade pavillions traveled to many countries, Bucky's name became known worldwide.

Fig. 7-8

a.

b.

As nomads have known for centuries, round shelters use the least material, are lightest, strongest, and withstand extreme weather. The North Face company was the first to exploit the structural advantages of true geodesic geometry in camping tents. These three photographs show several early prototypes being demonstrated to a very pleased Bucky Fuller.

Fig. 7-9

c.

This North Face VE 25 geodesic 4-season tent is in current production. With a 48-square-foot (6-square-meter) floor area, and a 52-inch (132-cm) height, the tent handles three people and their gear. It packs into a stuffsack 8 inches in diameter by 28 inches long (20 cm x 71 cm). Weight: 9 pounds, 4 ounces (4.2 kg). Larger models may be available on special order. North Face geodesic tents are often employed on expeditions where terrible weather is expected.

Fig. 7-10

Fig. 7-11 (a-d)

Pull outwards on the base, and the diameter of Chuck Hoberman's beautifully articulated geodesic dome expands from 4.5 feet (1.37 meters) to 18 feet (5.48 meters). Squeeze the base inwards to shrink the dome back to its original size. The dome expands as a growing turtle's shell does—enlarging the hexagons and pentagons, not by adding triangles. Its shape, connectivity, and stability remain the same throughout the transformation. Hoberman's complex computer analysis and cleverly machined detailing make folding domes practical at last. A model sphere using this principle is available, see Appendix B.

Chapter 8

The Garden of Eden

The very first usable outdoor dome was what Bucky called a "Garden of Eden," a transparent shell under which the inhabitants could control the weather. A Garden-of-Eden home provides more than it consumes, a strong move toward "sustainability." Your life becomes an integral part of the place. This version of a Dymaxion dwelling represents a radically different way of defining the word "home."

Indoors Outdoors

Imagine living outdoors indoors in a transparent dome, picking organically grown vegetables right in your kitchen, sleeping in a bed under luxuriant trees, or slung right beneath the opened apex, comfortable regardless of the weather outside. Your autonomous garden home is heated and cooled by the sun, which also provides electricity and heats water. Solar heat is stored in translucent water tanks that nurture edible fish, and furnish nutrient-rich "fish exhaust" irrigation for the plants. As a gesture toward historical authenticity, you might even have an apple tree and a serpent.

Your Garden of Eden captures, treats, and recycles its own water. Human and kitchen wastes are composted or purified into potable drinking water by "Living Machines" (® Ocean Arks, International)—miniature wetlands that process wastes by natural (odor-free) means. The plants provide the oxygen-rich, clean air of a forest. You could raise bananas all year, even in New England.

Fig. 8-1

Bucky's very first successful full-scale, covered geodesic dome was also the first "Garden-of-Eden" climate-controlling envelope. The inflated skin was short-lived polyethylene (there was nothing better available in 1949) over a spidery, foldable tube frame. Its rigidity amazed its student builders at Black Mountain College.

There is no connection to city power, water, or sewage systems. It is truly organic architecture.

You wake to dawnlight, watch rain-lashing storms without getting wet (unless you want to), enjoy the moon and stars on clear nights. Near-perfect acoustics bring particular pleasure to music-making and listening. There is time for contemplation and play because there are few maintenance chores. There is nothing that can rot or be eaten by termites, nothing to paint, nothing to replace, no gutters to clean. (You may have to weed, though.)

Fig. 8-2

Instead of being a static physical and psychological fortress guarding a museum of collected knickknacks, your Garden-of-Eden home is a stage upon which you act out your life. It changes as you do, and as the garden grows. You can change it to match your mood and needs. It lets you grow. It *encourages* you to grow.

And it is safe: There is no need to fear the most violent earthquakes or hurricanes, or even near-misses by tornados. Best of all, it costs less to build and run than a "normal" home. If purchased, it will be paid off like a car, in four or five years. If leased (the best choice), it will be automatically upgraded as the technology improves. Either way, you'll move in the same day you order it.

All of the above sounds like future-hype, but in fact, every feature mentioned has been field-tested and well-proven beyond any doubt, in a wide variety of climates. None of it requires exotic materials or processes, but occupants will need some knowledge to run it. (A CD loaded with the needed know-how combined with on-line advice would assist inexperienced occupants.) You could have a Garden-of-Eden home today if a suitable dome was available to house it.

The Autonomous Package consisted of all the furnishings and appliances for a family of six living unconnected to the public utility grid. Items were selected to pack into an 8 x 8 x 25-foot container that could ship in a small semitrailer or flatbed truck. As a mass-produced package, the items cost less than 10% of the individual retail prices. Bucky holds the model designed and built by students at the Chicago Institute of Design in 1949. The model box is transparent only to show the nested contents. Furniture and appliances specifically designed for this purpose would pack even smaller, and be better in every way. A suitable Garden-of-Eden dome cover for the Autonomous Package can be seen in the background. Fig. 8-5 brings it closer.

That assumes it is legal, which in most places in the United States, it is not. At many locations in our democracy, codes declare greenhouses as "unfit for human habitation!" I regard codes as a temporary problem, serious mostly because banks will not lend on unapproved buildings. History shows that codes can and will be changed when safety and utility have been proven by credible lab tests, and when there is sufficient public and commercial demand for the advantages. For example, automobiles were restricted to round, "sealed beam" headlamps starting about 1940. By 1980, it was demonstrated that unsealed halogen-bulb headlights improved aerodynamics and illumination. The mandatory sealed-beam specification was superceded by performance criteria. Building codes can be upgraded in the same way.

The first production Garden-of-Eden domes will probably be built and occupied in remote areas where codes do not apply. Carefully crafted media coverage will produce demand. The first step is to make some convincing, photogenic domes, and learn how to run them.

Designing a Garden-of-Eden home is an exercise in comprehensive thinking. The enclosing dome must perform structurally, and be energy and resource-efficient. It must provide nurturing conditions for people and plants. That means very tight control of the interior temperature, humidity, and air quality, independent of a variety of conditions outside. No substances that could pollute the indoor atmosphere or soil can be employed. Of course, the structure will have to be affordable to buy and to operate. It must last indefinitely, or at least until a superior model appears. Its lifetime energy use must be as low as possible. It should be recyclable.

What happens inside is up to you. Whereas the protective shell is made from high-tech materials, the interior can be local soil, stone, wood, or anything else that interests you. You could erect a dome over an interesting ruin. You could situate it on the flat roof of a highrise. None of the contents will be subject to weathering. Unlike a static floor plan chopped into irrevocable rooms, an interior that involves living things will always be changing according to the rhythms of season and genetics. Like any garden, things can be planted, transplanted, and rearranged. (Even a Dymaxion Bathroom could easily be moved.) Like any garden, it will never be finished. Life in a Garden-of-Eden will be an engaging process of continuous learning and exploration, rather than an endless stream of image-defending chores, and empty entertainment that ultimately induces lethargy and depression.

What would a neighborhood of Garden-of-Eden homes look like? Most homes reflect a choice from a limited list of architectural styles, inside and out. They vary only in detail, as if they were different brands of the same appliance. Domes may all look alike outside (as aircraft do, for instance), but their open interior space permits an unlimited range of quickly changed individual expression, independent of arbitrary styles and motifs.

Despite complaints that domes look "industrial," a Garden of Eden is actually more "natural" than any conventional home. True, the high-tech shell is probably not wood (though it could be). But, as Bucky pointed out, *any* material is made of natural elements. Furthermore, conventional houses are not as natural as they appear. Windows, paint, roofing, plumbing and wiring, lights, ducts, tile, concrete, brick, mirrors, insulation, sheetrock, countertops, rugs, appliances, and the heating and cooling equipment are all industrial products. A Garden of Eden dome would use less, or none, of these.

If the Garden-of-Eden has such potential, why have none been built? There have been many proposals; in fact, Bucky's first dome in 1949 was intended as one (Fig.8-1). The biggest obstacle has been the lack of affordable, permanent, transparent materials. Cutting glass into triangles is expensive, tricky (the triangle points are weak), and wasteful of material. The only long-lived rigid plastics are too expensive or too short-lived. Most plastic films are temporary and fragile.

Insulating a transparent dome has proved difficult. Double glazing eventually collects moisture between the panes, as can be seen in decaying patio doors. Two or more layers of rigid plastic collect uncleanoutable moisture, dirt, and unsightly algae between the layers. Inert gas fillings slowly leak away and usually cannot be recharged. Plastic films are eaten by sunlight or flap themselves into tatters in gales.

In 1970, a new design—the Pillowdome—utilized plastic in a new way that solved all of the above problems except limited longevity (see page 168). In 1982, that design was upgraded with a plastic film claimed to be permanent. Fifteen years of rigorous testing has proved it successful. Now, forty-six years after Bucky's first prototype, a Garden-of-Eden dome is both affordable and practical.

The hinged package on its way to becoming a 928-square-foot (86-square-meter) living space, about the size of a "Granny unit" today. The container wall sections become the floor, complete with factory-installed plumbing and wiring ready for use. Marked components and container panels would repack easily for moving.

Fig. 8-3

The completed package is displayed on a landscaped circle, ready for its climate-controlling geodesic dome. The dome components would accompany the Autonomous Package in the same truck, facilitating one-day installation on a prepared site. Because the hardware that would make the Autonomous Package autonomous had not yet been invented, only the space it was expected to need was included.

Another version of the Autonomous Package was called the Mechanical Wing. It was a small, pop-top trailer that held a fully installed kitchen, Dymaxion Bathroom, cogenerator set (to provide electricity and heat), and associated hardware. Parked and popped, it could provide mechanical amenities to any shelter.

Fig. 8-4

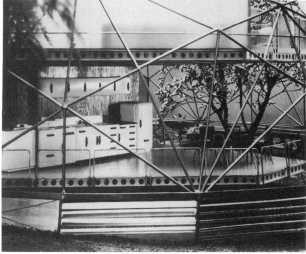

Fig. 8-5

These close-ups of the model behind Bucky in Fig. 8-2 give some idea of what a Garden-of-Eden dome might be like. The basic furnishings are from the Autonomous Package.

Skybreaks

Architecture departments in several universities turned their attention to Skybreak homes—houses without walls, sheltered by a transparent or translucent geodesic dome. It was an unfamiliar aesthetic, worth investigating. It was a safe opportunity to break with tradition. Bucky's students worked over the idea with imagination and vim that was unusual in a repressive time of Senator McCarthy's anti-Communist witch hunts.

Bucky's little transparent Garden-of-Eden dome at Black Mountain College (Fig. 8-1) encouraged fantasies of living close to nature while being protected from her occasional extremes of weather and biology. Students responded with imaginative designs that had few roots in the arbitrary styles of the past. Only the appliances and furniture were commonplace, and they might well have been more radical if architecture and product design departments had been on speaking terms in those postwar years.

The proposals came complete with convincing models and drawings (Figs. 8-6 to 8-13), but from what I could learn, no calculations were made for interior climate control, nor were there any investigations of greenhouse botany. Practicality depended upon technology and whole system design yet to come. No livable, full-size "Skybreak" dwellings were built at that time. (Architecture students could get a degree then without having ever built anything! In most schools, they still can.)

A number of transparent, but uninsulated, Skybreak dome-homes have been built and abandoned over the years since the student models shown here. Though beautiful, they required excessive heating and cooling to reduce

Jacks in the legs of this Skybreak allow it to be adjusted up and down for cooling and access. Bucky's MIT students made the model in 1952, but there was no practical way to try it full-scale. The car is Bucky's 1950 Kaiser proposal (Fig. 4-21). This Skybreak model was shown at New York's Museum of Modern Art.

extreme temperature swings that would otherwise have made them unsuitable for year-round occupation. They were actually nothing more than nineteenth century glass houses with a new aesthetic. The British found out long ago that living in your greenhouse could be unpleasant and expensive most of the year.

Lacking the materials to do better, Skybreak development stalled. Over time, the Garden-of-Eden concept has taken its place with a more comprehensive and systemic design that goes far beyond an arbitrary aesthetic. Today, the word "skybreak" usually refers to a skinless, geodesic dome framework used principally as a dramatic decoration.

The student Skybreak investigations did not produce an occupiable abode, but they did provide an inspiring, believable, and very attractive alternative to "tickytacky" tract houses and mobile homes. Alternatives take time to take hold. We'll see something like them yet.

Fig. 8-6

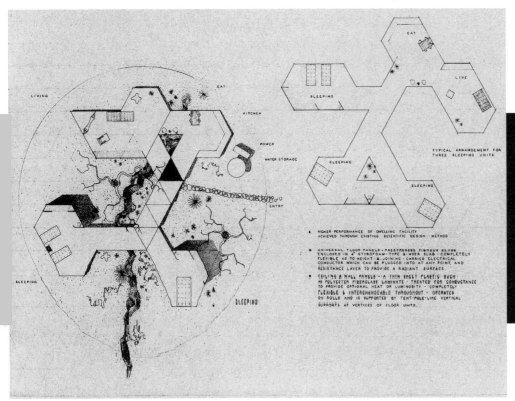

MIT students explored many schemes for Skybreak Dwellings in the early 1950s. This plan separates the rooms in a star pattern to give privacy and a selection of solar exposures.

Fig. 8-7

This drawing shows what the plan in Fig. 8-7 would look like when built. These proposals depend upon the "chilling machine" effect to keep the house cool, but no full-scale scientific tests were made to see if it would work in a transparent dome. Subsequent experience shows that overheating can be prevented. Recent experiments with Heat Mirror® indicate that actual cooling may be possible. The chilling effect cools opaque domes well.

Fig. 8-8

This Skybreak plan keeps the walled area compact and provides shade for the sleeping area.

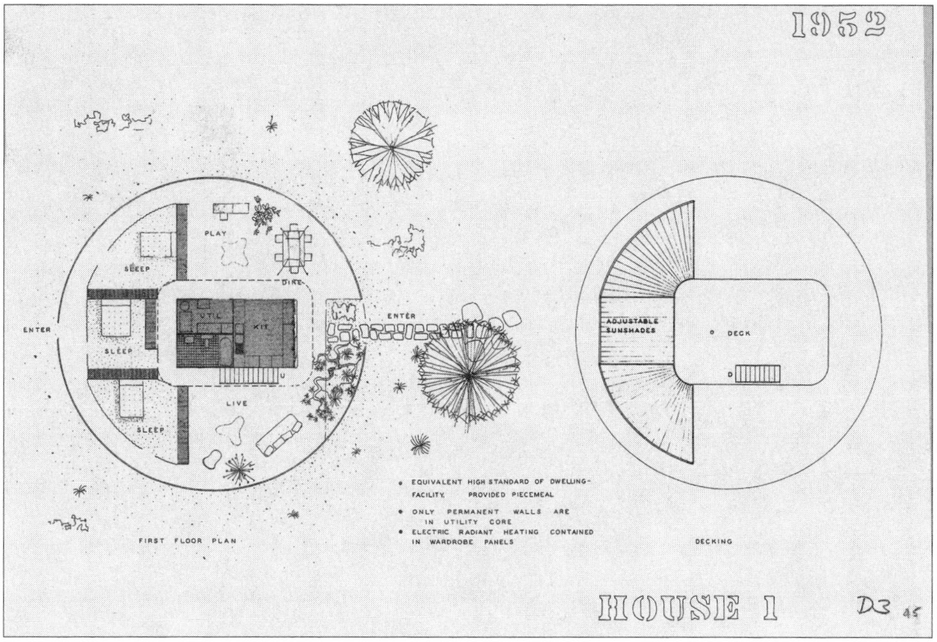

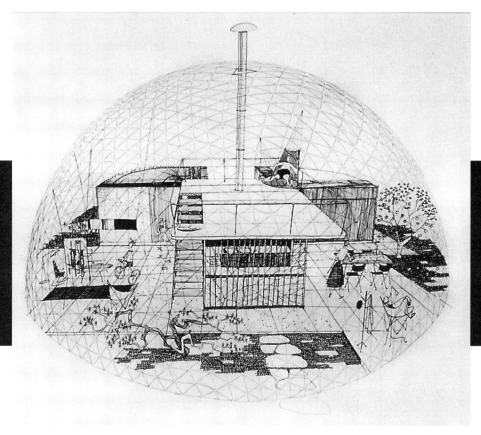

Fig. 8-9

A drawing based on the plan in Fig. 8-9. Recent students have suggested using a sleeping tower under openable triangles at the top of the dome, like those shown in Fig. 8-24.

Fig. 8-10

Fig. 8-11

This imaginative layout uses a transparent dome to cover what amounts to a conventional house without roof or most walls. This idea could also be applied to a partially dismantled obsolete home, bringing it solar heating and a drastically changed ambience.

This is another view of the model in Fig. 8-11.

Fig. 8-12

Here, two small domes cover the needed space. Though geodesic domes are cheaper per unit area and volume as they get bigger, smaller units would be more economical if they were in mass-production. This is essentially the same logic as the Dymaxion Deployment Units discussed in Chapter 2.

Fig. 8-13

An Airstream® trailer nestles in the shelter of a diaphanous 16-frequency, 20-foot (6-meter) dome made from 125 pounds (57 kg) of welded wire. With a transparent or translucent skin, a dome used in this way would provide climate-controlled surroundings for trailers, mobile homes, and other thermally inefficient buildings that are difficult to retrofit with better insulation. It was made by Don Richter, who later founded Temcor, the most prolific manufacturer of large commercial geodesic domes.

Fig. 8-14

The 175-foot (53-meter) diameter Climatron houses a tropical botanical garden. Except for the extreme humidity, it is easy to imagine living in there. It is still the best example of the "Garden of Eden" dome that Bucky envisaged, but by today's standards, the 1960 uninsulated structure uses excessive energy for heating and cooling. Modern materials and building techniques would improve efficiency. This dome is worth going out of your way to see. It's in St. Louis, MO.

Fig. 8-15

Fig. 8-16

After you've been in the Climatron for a few minutes, the structure attracts no more of your attention than does the sky when you're outdoors. The dome frame members have built-in gutters to direct drips and leaks. Humidity and condensation would need to be reduced for use as a living space—a problem that has so far resisted an energy-efficient solution. A number of experimenters are working on this; solar dehumidifiers are probably the answer. (We'll see.) Bucky generally left such details to other investigators, a practice that sometimes delayed progress when problems unexpectedly turned out to be inherent in his designs.

Montreal

Designed and realized by architect Shoji Sadao, Bucky's enormous Montreal dome was an utterly daring way to demonstrate the power of synergetics to millions of people. Nobody, including Bucky, had ever done anything like it before. It was, and is, a new experience for anyone venturing inside. Go see for yourself.

The great dome was built as the United States pavilion for the Expo 67 fair. The rather ordinary display inside was thoroughly overshadowed by the stunning 250-foot (76.2-meter) diameter structure glittering day and night like an enormous jewel. (Fig. 8-17). The light, open interior was in great contrast to the cumbersome architecture of most other fair displays. (Its only rival was Frei Otto's dramatic tension structure over the West German pavilion.)

A passenger monorail ran right through the dome well above the floor, bringing to mind the florid science fiction illustrations of glass cities on distant planets. To monorail riders, it looked as if the future had come early.

Bucky's original proposal was a dome nearly twice the size of the one that was finally built. It was to contain an animated version of his long-recommended Geoscope, complete with facilities for playing World Game® at a scale large enough to convince thousands of spectators that the world could work for everyone. (See Chapter 10). Shortsighted bean-counters won the day, choosing instead to build a smaller and cheaper version for a lackluster exhibit. To save a few dollars, the dome was built without the bolted construction that would have allowed it to be sold (at a profit) and moved when the fair was over.

Years later, the skin burned off in an unfortunate, easily preventable welder's fire that left the frame scorched, but undamaged. (Fig. 8-20). When the refurbished, but unskinned, dome reopened in 1995 as La Biosphère environmental education center, Montreal citizens gave it a warm welcome. They regard it as a symbol of their progressive city. It stands as a visible celebration of the otherwise invisible coordinates of Universe.

Fig. 8-17

The 250-foot (76.2-meter) dome housing the United States pavilion at Montreal's "Expo 67" gave a hint of what a Dymaxion neighborhood, office building, or factory might look like. Note the darkened monorail about to enter the dome near the lower left center. It was a dramatic ride, especially at night. The commonplace interior cost far more than the dome itself.

Pillowdomes

The Pillowdome concept arrived in 1969 in an unexpected, fully detailed dream, complete with bolts and nuts in the correct sizes. Transparent, insulated, and cheap, it is a practical embodiment of the Garden of Eden Bucky envisioned in 1949. I awoke, sketched it quickly, and commenced work without making a model first. (Bucky recommended having a pad and pencil always at hand—especially next to your bed. You have only a few minutes to get ideas and dreams onto paper before they are irretrievably lost.)

The first Pillowdome prototype was a 20-foot (6-meter) diameter dome framed in "EMT" electrical conduit, and skinned with triangular, inflated vinyl "pillows" sealed in a local shop that made inflatable toys (of all sorts). Because tubing and vinyl are made in continuous processes, a Pillowdome can be made with little or no waste. The size of this prototype was chosen as the largest that could be made without ordering custom-cut materials. Total waste was less than 3 pounds (1.36 kg) of vinyl snippets and tube cutoffs. (Fig. 8-22)

Full-size, live trees accented the unfamiliar feeling of a large, open, light, indoor space. The concave, hexagonal acrylic skin panels broke up sound waves, making normal conversation easy despite 5000 occupants all talking at once.

Fig. 8-18

Fig. 8-19

Disaster! A careless welder repeatedly ignited the multi-bulged acrylic skin, which finally burned slowly, but uncontrollably, when all the extinguishers were used up. Fire hoses couldn't reach twenty stories high. The dome had no sprinkler system because building codes based on unrealistic testing had mistakenly rated acrylic sufficiently fire-retardant for such use. There were no injuries, and the geodesic framework was not damaged. Bucky was dismayed. He'd dedicated the magnificent structure to his wife, Anne.

Fig. 8-20

The light-colored star patterns above the U.S.A. display are triangular, automatic roller shades that were supposed to deploy or furl as directed by a computer. On the first day, their operating cables twisted, leaving all of the shades permanently and untidily jammed in the random positions you see here. As happens so often, bureaucratic budget-cutting was the underlying cause of this embarrassing, unnecessary failure. Bucky was disgusted; the cable he specified would have worked fine. (He knew about cables and sheaves from decades of sailing.) Innovations need special effort to ensure the convincing, flawless performance needed for credibility and acceptance.

Handsomely repainted, but unskinned, the great dome is now known as La Biosphère, an interactive environmental education center of advanced design. An observation deck gives a wonderful view of the area. The dome remains a popular Montreal landmark and tourist attraction.

Fig. 8-21

The first Pillowdome worked as planned, with no serious problems. Bucky immediately recognized it as "the first of the second generation of geodesic domes," and ordered one for Bear Island, the Fuller family's retreat off the coast of Maine. Six more were made and tested. The project temporarily ceased when vinyl was reported toxic to its production workers. Vinyl also smells bad and has a limited lifespan. The dome on Bear Island lasted six years before succumbing to the inevitable Brown Death suffered by aged convertible back windows. It successfully withstood heavy snow loads and several hurricanes, despite being built with a zero safety factor to reveal any weaknesses.

Work restarted eight years later at the New Alchemy Institute in Falmouth, MA. The famed environmental research center (now disbanded) needed a replacement for a deteriorating wood-and-fiberglass dome (Fig. 8-26). About the same time, DuPont announced its Tefzel® film, a stronger derivative of the Teflon® found in no-stick frying pans. Made for battery plate separators and wire insulation in spaceships, Tefzel is one of the very few plastics that does not deteriorate in sunlight or other cosmic rays. It is almost chemically inert, odorless, and does not exude or absorb toxic fumes. It is tough—a 60 pound (27.2 kg) pull will not enlarge a knife slit in 5-mil (5 thousands-of-an-inch) (0.127-mm) material. We made a respectable trampoline out of it!

Tefzel has an important bonus for Pillowdome use: It is transparent to sunlight, and it stays that way. Dirt, snow, vandals' paint, and just about anything else you can name will not stick to it. Because it can be used in thin layers, a Tefzel panel transmits more solar energy than an equivalent glass panel.

The improved Pillowdome prototype (it's the second of the proverbial three it takes to get anything right) uses a recycled geodesic aluminum water pipe frame originally designed by Starnet International Corporation's president, Wendel R. Wendel. A production version could benefit from custom aluminum or pultruded carbon fiber that could ease assembly and provide a "thermal break" that would eliminate the need for frame insulation in cold climates.

The inflatable, triangular Tefzel pillows are thermally welded gas-tight (using special equipment) all around, several inches inboard of their edges. The resulting flaps are secured to the frame, "shingled" downhill, by means of riveted-on, semi-cylindrical clamp strips. Foam-filled aluminum covers insulate and squeeze the overlapped flaps water and wind-tight where they come together at the hubs. (The covers are Sigg brand camping pot lids. "Never make items you can buy off the shelf," was another Bucky lesson.)

Fig. 8-22

Thermally welded, gas-tight triangular pillows accommodate expansion and contraction, and don't flutter or flap in hurricane winds. Nonflammable argon fill insulates better than air, and suppresses flame if fire ruptures a pillow. The bulges suppress annoying echo effects found in other domes. The caulkless, overlapping pillow attachment system doesn't leak. In fact, it cannot leak (which is different), even in horizontal rain.

This dome was originally intended to have its thickly-padded living space floor at the top edge of the translucent lower triangles. The floor would normally be completely clear of partitions and belongings. When desired, furnishings and kitchen appliances would fold out of the floor like the back seats of station wagons. The waterbed would lurk under a trapdoor, ready for action. The idea was to have commandable space that could be transformed into whatever you desired: house-as-stage-set, instead of house-as-museum. Testing in everyday use showed this 20-foot (6-meter) dome to be a bit small for the scheme. Stage-set living should work well in a larger one.

This results in a permanently watertight dome skin that does not depend on caulk or sun-degradable gaskets. Because the inflated pillows can stretch a little, the sealing is not affected by expansion and contraction.

Inflation to just 1/2 pound per square inch (0.0352 kg per square centimeter) pressure bulges the pillows tight, preventing the material from flapping itself to death in the wind. The resilient pillows have successfully repelled kicks, bricks, flying branches, hail, enemy BBs, pencil pokes, and hoehandles. Small knife wounds can be easily patched. Entire pillows can be replaced by one person in less than an hour. The pillows are inflated with nontoxic, nonflammable argon gas. It insulates better than air, and will act as a fire extinguisher if a pillow is melted by flames. In pragmatically realistic fire tests, the thin Tefzel pillows disappeared without visible smoke instead of burning.

Inventor (and sole patent holder), Charles Hall contributed his first waterbed to the first Pillowdome. Always a sailor, Bucky had to give it a try. (He approved.) The interesting trapeze above it doesn't show in this view.

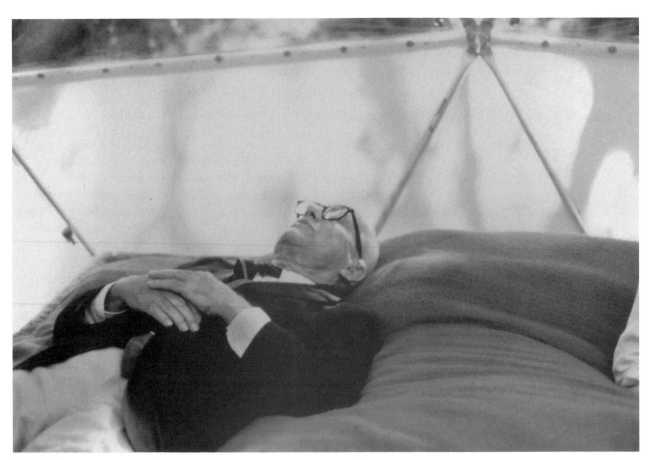

Fig. 8-23

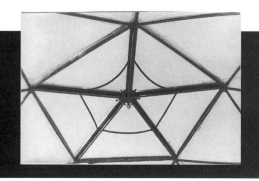

Releasing a single rope allows springs to open the top pentagon. It would be a simple matter to open an entire dome in this manner, enabling occupants to be outdoors indoors in a few seconds. Birds colliding with the pillows are unhurt—they just bounce off.

Fig. 8-24

Fig. 8-25

The first Pillowdome, with its vents in the Lotus Position. In a transparent dome, the "chilling machine" effect (Chapter 5) will prevent the interior from getting any hotter than outdoor ambient temperature, but it won't feel cool. With its vents closed, the dome captures diffuse solar heat well, even on cold cloudy days. Interior temperatures hover around 75° F (23.8° C) when it is 40° F (4.4° C) outside. Night temperatures depend on solar heat storage capacity. Recent computer simulations show that simple changes could significantly improve the already good performance.

Fig. 8-26

This wood-framed, double-glazed fiberglass dome developed fatal rot and opaque green algae growth when only five years old. Condensation that accumulated between the skins was the problem. Despite severe biodegradation, demolition proved more difficult than anticipated; the dome had to be beaten apart with sledgehammers.

Critics correctly complain that aluminum and Tefzel are high-tech materials that require distressing amounts of energy to manufacture. But the 31-foot (9.4-meter) Pillowdome employs about 400 pounds (181 kg) of these materials to cover 755 square feet (70 square meters). The materials apparently do not degrade, are certainly not edible, and require no maintenance. The dome is so efficient thermally that its total lifetime energy costs for construction and operation are much less than other designs made from more politically correct materials. It is also hurricane-and earthquake-proof, and tornado-resistant.

At this writing, the Pillowdome is probably the strongest, lightest, permanent transparent building yet devised. With a total of 0.012 inch (0.3 mm) of material between indoors and out, the Pillowdome may be regarded as a gesture toward ephemeralization. It may also be the first greenhouse designed to the nearest angstrom to match the needs of the plants inside. It represents a new sort of marriage between high-technology and biology.

The assembly crew easily supports the top half of the dome while the lower triangles are attached. The completed 31-foot (9.4-meter) diameter structure weighs about 400 pounds (181 kg), light enough to let it be carried to another location years later, without disassembly. A small station wagon delivered all the parts in one load. Dome-lite.

Fig. 8-27

The project made use of information gathered by dozens of investigators over forty-six years. A surprising number of them respected and made use of Bucky's ideas. No competition was involved—the work has gone ahead cooperatively at its own gestation rate, just as Bucky had said it would. The work of ecologists, biologists, ictheologists, engineers, designers, computer programmers, organizers, and fund-raisers, reinforced one another synergetically in unexpected ways—also as he said they would if you were working for the good of everyone.

Bucky liked the result. At the opening ceremony, he said, "This is how I knew it could be," and admonished the sponsors present to fund instrumentation for further tests. DuPont generously did so.

The Pillowdome has another attribute that may not be obvious at first glance. New Alchemy researchers found that the New England states import more than 90% of their food and energy. The money leaves the region—one reason for widespread poverty in those states. Year-round food raising in short-lived, high-maintenance commercial greenhouses heated by fossil fuel is too expensive, but properly designed solar Pillowdomes could raise vegetables and fresh fish locally all year.

The food-raising Pillowdomes would be light enough to be installed on the flat roofs of downtown highrise buildings. In fact, the Pillowdome was intentionally designed with that in mind. Newly developed lightweight soil or hydroponics keep the total weight well within the code-meeting capabilities of office buildings and apartments. City farming thus becomes a reasonable enterprise. It's an idea that's been talked about for twenty years. As this is written, several groups are working to make it real.

The Pillowdome at the (now defunct) New Alchemy Institute on Cape Cod, MA, has withstood severe hurricane winds, deep snow loads, vandalism, and occasional neglect for fourteen years. It is the second prototype. The third prototype, now being designed, will address the annoying condensation that sometimes occurs (it's not inside the sealed pillows) and a few details that will facilitate mass production.

The first commercial Pillowdome use may be as covers for the solar-driven "Living Machines"® indoor wetlands sewage treatment plants being built in increasing numbers by Ocean Arks International. Old-mode building and zoning codes must change before Pillowdomes can be used as homes; in most communities in our democracy, greenhouses have arbitrarily been deemed "unfit for human habitation." Tenants may be subject to eviction by armed sheriffs.

Fig. 8-28

Fig. 8-29

Those are tomatoes, madam. Hundreds of visitors came to learn about the Pillowdome and other biological explorations at the New Alchemy Institute. Fiberglass fish tanks store solar heat, and release it at night to maintain the desired temperature. They also provide crops with nitrogen-rich "fish exhaust" irrigation water. Locally obtained dark algae in the tanks feeds a population of tilapia, mirror carp (gefilte fish fish), and catfish, and captures solar energy most efficiently for local conditions. The balance of plants, fish, and solar heating was worked out by the New Alchemists ten years before the famous, more complex, and much more expensive Biosphere II experiment in Arizona. Widespread commercial use of large vegetable and fish-growing Pillowdomes could significantly improve local economies by reducing their need to export money for food.

This 50-foot biodome stood at the Windstar Foundation in Snowmass, CO, before being moved to Prescott, AZ. Calculations were done by Bucky's colleague, Amy C. Edmondson, author of *A Fuller Explanation* (1987, Birkhauser); John Katzenberger and friends designed the details, made the parts, and put it up. It is double-glazed with polycarbonate panels. Note the octet truss decks. With a few modifications, this sort of dome could serve as a home or office. As with the Pillowdome, it will take a few more prototypes (and some "test-pilot" occupants) to perfect it as a Garden-of-Eden living space.

Fig. 8-31

The plants are cozy and warm in there! Morning sun soon slides snow off the slippery dome even in cloudy weather. The three-layer pillows are DuPont Tefzel®, proved to last at least thirty years in tropical sun. (Actual life is unknown.) The tough, odorless plastic film doesn't absorb or exude toxic substances. Like Teflon®, dirt will not stick to it. A middle layer of the Heat Mirror® featured in the best high-performance windows would reduce heat loss at night.

Unlike glass, Tefzel transmits all wavelengths needed by plants to grow, plus ultraviolet light that suppresses black sooty mold and other diseases that thrive in glass greenhouses. There's more light in a Pillowdome anyway— structural members shadow just 4% of the growing area, all day long. A typical conventional greenhouse casts a 22% shadow on the floor. Biosphere II casts almost 40% shadow at certain times—slowing plant growth enough to reduce the production of oxygen required by humans and domestic animals.

Fig. 8-30

Senior Eden: a 300-foot (91.4-meter) Pillowdome sits on a raised berm with 35 earth-sheltered senior citizen's apartments in its perimeter, designed by Malcolm Wells. Back doors face the street. Front doors face the huge community garden which provides most vegetables, oxygenated air, and interesting work for seniors who are able and willing. The sun provides heat, hot water, and electricity, greatly reducing utility bills. Fish tanks store heat, provide table fish, and deliver nutrients to the plants. (For clarity, fewer are shown than would be needed.) Daytime temperatures would be comfortable all year in most climates. A rigorous cost analysis by New Alchemists John Todd and John Wolfe shows that this structure could be built for less than conventional apartments without gardens.

Fig 8-32

Chapter 9

Megastructures

*The social and environmental costs of conventional cities and towns
are too high. Of course, Bucky had some solutions. . .*

When Bucky was young, filthy, decaying cities, were unhealthy, unpleasant
places to live and work. Suburbs were seen as the answer. Only a few critics—
Lewis Mumford, for example—saw that pretty suburbia would not be much
better in the long run. It would take many years before it was clear to most
people that sprawling urban development eats money and land, expensively
disrupting existing communities and natural systems. Many people still do not
understand how urban sprawl is connected to crime, disease, disenchantment,
pollution, and other problems. In many—but not all—countries, sprawl is
considered inevitable and unstoppable.

A small number of entrepreneurs (who often live elsewhere) stand to gain by
uncontrolled growth. Their destructive developments are heavily and invisibly
subsidized by tax money—often from the very people who will bear the brunt
of the damage. Laws and public opinion have been manipulated to permit,
and even encourage, the wasteful and destructive practice.

As the true costs of suburbia became obvious, Bucky began to seek other
ways of arranging housing. His autonomous Dymaxion House and efficient
Dymaxion automobile were solutions that could well *increase* sprawl by making
it cheaper and easier to flee from the city. On the other hand, most cities were

so thoroughly obsolete in function and hardware that renovation was absurdly expensive and essentially futile. Realizing this, Bucky and other architects (Le Corbusier, for instance) offered proposals featuring high-density, resource-efficient housing and workspace for thousands of people.

There are several ways to approach this goal. Most common is the megastructure —a one-building town. The idea is not new. A road trip to Alaska will take you past many "towns" consisting of a single, funky building that simultaneously serves as a gas station, motel, restaurant, general store, bar, repair garage, bait shop, public telephone, school bus stop, post office, kennel, and quarters for the folks running the show. These agglomerations all look about the same for good reason: Tough conditions and expensive supplies cause people to think clearly, if not elegantly. They intuitively put everything under one roof over a small plot of land. Total loss in the event of a fire is the only serious disadvantage.

Old Man River's City

Bucky worked out the calculations for several megastructures. Old Man River's City, intended to replace East St, Louis, IL, is the best-known.

Fig. 9-1

Fig. 9-2

These hazy photos are of a model showing the general layout of Old Man River's City, a mile-diameter (1500 meter) megastructure providing the homes, workspaces, and re-creation area for 125,000 people. The enormous dome is supported 1000 feet (3005 meters) above a "moon-crater" depression with a raised rim. The outer surface of the rim is terraced to provide 25,000 earth-sheltered garden homes, each with a view and a generous 2500 square feet (232.24 square meters) of floor area.

The inner surface of the crater is terraced for communal use. Millions of square feet of commercial space share the hollowed-out earth of the crater's rim with parking lots and services. Weather under the dome would always be pleasant despite the sometimes-unpleasant East St. Louis climate. (I have not seen the calculations for tornado-resistance.)

Old Man River's City is intended to replace the poverty-stricken, hopelessly obsolete city of East St. Louis, IL. Bucky specifically recommended that government money *not* be sought, for it always comes with a grievous burden of interest which eventually saps the local economy for the benefit of banks and other parasitic operators. To the organizers' credit, they refused millions of dollars saddled with restrictions that would have compromised the project.

Bucky wanted the entire effort to come from the people in-volved. Decades have passed with no construction, but work continues. Organizers held a Syntegration (see Chapter 10) in early 1995. Some real progress in financing was made. Enormous projects need a long gestation. Old Man River's City may happen yet.

Triton City

Whatever their design, megastructures on land always involve huge expenditures for renting land or renting the money (at exorbitant interest rates) to buy the land. Natural habitat is inevitably destroyed. A floating megastructure needs no land, construction earthmoving, landscaping, or road net. A properly designed floating city would have little direct environmental impact. Bucky designed two types. One is a collection of geodesic, spherical submarine chambers anchored deep, below the effects of wave action. Only access shafts would show above water. The sub-cities could act as docking and cargo transfer facilities for freight-carrying submarines, providing a worldwide cargo-handling system unaffected by weather or season. The submarine system would be expensive, however, and subject to the never-ending threat of disaster caused by corrosion, mechanical failure, or fire—just like a military submarine. A city floating on the surface would be safer and cheaper.

Triton City was designed as a private Japanese venture for communities that would float in Tokyo Bay. With the center of buoyancy below the deepest wave action, the floating cities and their 100,000 inhabitants would be immune to earthquakes and tidal waves. The U.S. Department of Housing and Urban Development (HUD), and the U.S. Navy analyzed the scheme and pronounced it practical socially, economically, and structurally. With no land cost burden, rents could be held just above poverty level, providing truly low-cost housing with a high level of amenities.

Some people have wondered why Bucky used a tetrahedron as the basis for the 5000-person module. In contrast to a dome, a tetrahedron has the most surface (and thus material) to cover the least volume—hardly an example of efficiency. But in this case, surface area is what Bucky wanted. The inhabitants were not to be housed *in* the Triton unit, the apartments were located *on* the terraced surface where each could have a view. The pyramidal shape would assure stability by keeping the centers of gravity and wind pressure low. The slanted facades would ease servicing and maintenance, and make fatal falls from balconies unlikely. Facilities not requiring a view would be inside, out of sight. The relatively small modules would allow the project to grow incrementally to match the need and the money available. Commutes would be short—perhaps just a walk down a gangplank into the business district. The concept makes a lot of sense.

Fig. 9-3

An Outrageous Postcard

A third possibility for a megastructure is to cover existing buildings or groups of buildings, a task that would not be reasonable without the several advantages of geodesic domes.

AIR VIEW OF NEW YORK CITY WITH ITS SKYSCRAPERS

Completely surrounded by water, Manhattan presents unusual docking facilities for a great city. The largest ships from all over the world have their docks less than one mile from the midtown area. Hudson River Palisades can be seen in the distance.

IN FOREGROUND 3/4 MILE DIAMETER ⅓ HEMI-SPHERICAL GEODESIC DOME OVER LOWER MANHATTAN ALTITUDE AT ZENITH 2234 FEET

address

IN BACKGROUND 1¼ MILE DIAMETER ¼ QUARTER SPHERICAL GEODESIC DOME OVER MIDTOWN MANHATTAN FROM 28ᵗʰ ST. TO 55ᵗʰ ST AND FROM NINE AVE TO SECOND AVE. INCLUDING ALL LARGE BUILDINGS AS WELL AS PENNSYLVANIA STA AND GRAND CENTRAL — MADISON SQUARE GARDEN BROADWAY THEATER DISTRICT AND NEW MADISON AND THIRD AVE AND PARK AVE SKYSCRAPERS. ALTITUDE AT ZENITH -3580 FEET.

PUBLISHED BY HERBCO CARD CO., 49-19 27TH AVE., WOODSIDE L. I., N.Y.

Bucky couldn't resist scrawling this postcard with his proposal to cover substantial portions of Manhattan. The transparent, climate-controlling weather shields would act as "chilling machines" (See Chapter 5, Chilled Domes) to relieve New York's notorious, stifling summer heat. In winter, solar gain and wind deflection would produce balmy weather inside the buildings and in the streets, substantially reducing the need to individually heat inefficient buildings. Bucky calculated the dome's total skin surface would be less than 5% of the total wall and roof area of the buildings it covered, giving immense thermal advantage.

The project is technically and economically feasible; geodesic domes get stronger as they get bigger, and domes of this size would get additional pneumatic support from the air inside (see Fig. 9-5). Much of the slim structural network would be too far above the street to be visible. Bucky calculated that saved energy and the elimination of expensive snow removal would quickly pay for the domes. Of course, vehicles and businesses would have to be nonpolluting.

The drastic proposal may be extreme, but it does get you thinking. That's just what Bucky had in mind.

Fig.9-4

Cloud Nine

Cloud Nine is probably possible, but even Bucky didn't expect to see one soon. He offered it as a jarring exercise, intended to stimulate the imaginative thinking we're going to need if the billions of new Earth citizens predicted to arrive soon are to have decent housing.

Like floating and underwater cities, this fantastic proposal avoided the economic and environmental costs of using land for housing. Bucky envisioned buoyant, "Cloud Nine" tensegrity spheres a mile (1.6 km) or more in diameter sheltering autonomous communities of several thousand people.

What would keep them airborne? A straightforward surface-to-volume calculation shows that the structural weight of a half-mile (0.8 km) diameter sphere would be one-thousandth of the weight of the air inside. When trapped solar energy and human activity heated the air inside just one degree above the surrounding air temperature, even an unskinned sphere would float like a huge hot-air balloon. A skinned, one-mile (1.6 km) diameter sphere could easily support itself and several thousand people and their goods, day or night.

Cloud Nines could be anchored to mountaintops, with inhabitants traveling to the ground or other Cloud Nines by photovoltaically powered aircraft based on the work of Dr. Paul MacReady. The sky cities could also be permitted to drift at a preferred altitude, enabling their populations to see the world, or even to migrate like birds.

Bucky expected Cloud Nines would appear far in the future as one component of the hardware that would enable humans to "converge and deploy around Earth without its depletion."

Fig. 9-5

1,500 AD - 1840 AD

The best average speed of horse drawn coaches on land
and sailing ships at sea was approximately 10 m.p.h.

Chapter 10

Spaceship Earth

In reality, I have not left home. My backyard has just grown bigger.
Now the world is my backyard.—RBF

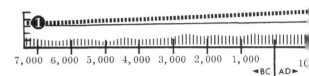

7,000 6,000 5,000 4,000 3,000 2,000 1,000   1(
◄BC │ AD►

It's a One-Town World

Isaac Newton's sense of "normal" was to be at rest. To him, Universe was
a sculpture. It was *The* Universe. Bucky noted sadly that adherents to the
"Big Bang" theory are still caught in Newtonian thought: They regard
Universe as an "it."

In contrast to Newton, Einstein's "normal" was the speed of light and other
radiation. His Universe was made up of nonsimultaneous energy events.
What we think of as real may not be there: Light from the North Star takes
640 years to get here. To Einstein (and to Bucky, who knew and admired
him), Universe is a continuously changing scenario, unknowable except in
principle, and in localized special cases. Because of this, Bucky liked to say,
"Truth is always approximate," or "Truth is a tendency." Universe will always
defy "thinkaboutability" to some extent. Process and direction are more
important than goals.

Nothing is standing still, not even here on Earth. A person "at rest" on the
equator is whizzing along at 1000 miles per hour (1609 kph) as Earth rotates
on its axis. At the same time, Earth is speeding around the sun at 60,000

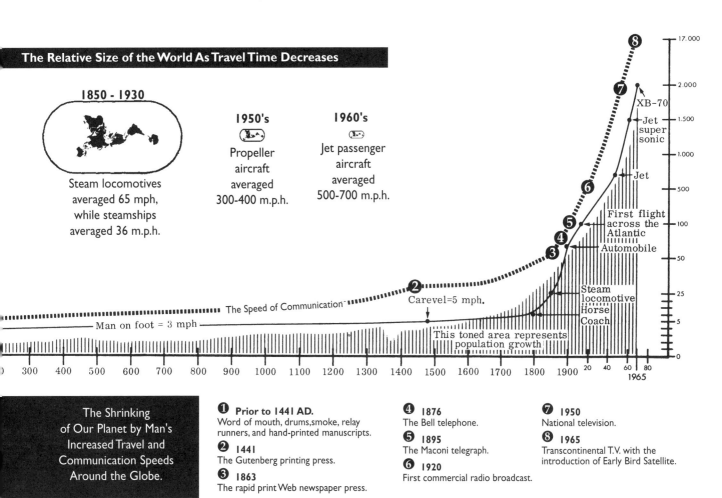

The Relative Size of the World As Travel Time Decreases

1850 - 1930
Steam locomotives averaged 65 mph, while steamships averaged 36 m.p.h.

1950's
Propeller aircraft averaged 300-400 m.p.h.

1960's
Jet passenger aircraft averaged 500-700 m.p.h.

The Shrinking of Our Planet by Man's Increased Travel and Communication Speeds Around the Globe.

❶ **Prior to 1441 AD.**
Word of mouth, drums, smoke, relay runners, and hand-printed manuscripts.

❷ **1441**
The Gutenberg printing press.

❸ **1863**
The rapid print Web newspaper press.

❹ **1876**
The Bell telephone.

❺ **1895**
The Maconi telegraph.

❻ **1920**
First commercial radio broadcast.

❼ **1950**
National television.

❽ **1965**
Transcontinental T.V. with the introduction of Early Bird Satellite.

YEAR	500,000 BC	20,000 BC	300 BC	500 AD	1500 AD	1900 AD	1925 AD	1950 AD	1965 AD
Required time to travel around the globe	A few hundred thousand years	A few thousand years	A few hundred years	A few tens of years	A few years	A few months	A few weeks	A few days	A few hours
Means of transportation	Human on foot over ice bridges	On foot and by canoe	Canoe with small sail or paddles or relays of runners	Large sail boats with oars, pack animals, and horse chariots	Big sailing ships (with compass), horse teams, and coaches	Steam boats and railroads, (Suez and Panama Canals)	Steamships, transcontinental railways, autos, and airplanes	Steamships, railways, auto, jet and rocket aircraft	Atomic steamships, high speed railways, auto, and rocket-jet aircraft
Distance per day (land)	15 miles	15-20 miles	20 miles	15-25 miles	20-25 miles	Rail 300-900 miles	Rail 400-900 miles	Rail 500-1,500 miles	Rail 1,000-2,000 miles
Distance per day (sea or air)		20 miles by sea	40 miles by sea	135 miles by sea	175 miles by sea	250 miles by sea	3,000-6,000 miles by air	6,000-9,500 miles by air	408,000 miles by air
Potential State size	None	A small valley in the vicinity of a small lake	Small part of a continent	Large area of a continent with coastal colonies	Great parts of a continent with transoceanic colonies	Full continents and transocean comonwealth	Full continents and transocean Commonwealths	The Globe	The Globe and more

Fig. 10-1

Bucky drew this chart in 1965. The numbers assume state-of-the-art capability at that time. Predictions based on these curves have proved to be very close to what has happened since this was prepared.

miles per hour (96,558 kph). Our solar system is speeding through the galaxy, and the galaxy is speeding through space, at unimaginable speeds. Closer to home, we are increasingly speeding around on the surface of our planet as we become world beings.

The first Earth people were bunched together for survival. Then they scattered across the globe to live under various trying conditions. Those conditions caused what we mistakenly call "races" to evolve. Now people are coming back together. Bucky said that this was part of a vast plan for us. He said it must be a divine plan because there seems to be a very strong tendency for humanity to become one people, even though there is no organized effort to bring this about. It's just happening.

Until very recently, the average human walked everywhere. (A brave few ventured upon the sea.) Many walkers never went further than the horizon during their lifetime. Bucky estimated that an average pedestrian covers about 1100 miles (1770 km) annually. By World War I, a typical citizen of an industrial nation still walked that distance, but added another 1100 miles by auto or train. World War II raised that to 1100 on foot and 10,000 miles a year by mechanical means, with a significant number of people travelling 50,000-100,000 miles a year.

The average U.S. family moves about every three years. (Statistics vary from one-and-a-half years to five years, depending whether military families are included.) How long have you been at your present address? When Bucky asked audiences that question, it usually turned out that the great majority had occupied their present home for less than five years. The demographics of cities is changing to accommodate air travel. We are on the move.

As people get around more ("increase their sweepout," in Bucky's phrase), the world is apparently shrinking. (Fig. 10-1). The literacy rate for all people hovers around 90%. Satellite broadcasting brings news and programs from all, to all, through wireless radio and TV. The commonly held knowledge undermines local authority (including parental authority). The Internet laces together its millions of users (mostly in English) in a manner that would startle A. G. Bell. English is well on the way to becoming the first or second language of most of the world's citizens. English is becoming the first world language.

Credit cards and telephone cards now work in the major cities of most countries, and the outback in many. The dollar is acceptable nearly everywhere—if not officially, then on the street. It may become the first world currency.

Weights and measures, regulations for safety and pollution, industrial standards, travel protocols, music, movies, video and electronic communication compatibility, all are tending to international agreement. Shared technology unites peoples—especially their young. The world's young are beginning to stir. Bucky thought that young people were our only hope.

Tourism is the largest business in the world. Millions of people visit virtually every country and region for business, pleasure, or mere curiosity. The improved efficiency of enormous aircraft now on the drawing boards will likely bring a drop in air fares. Airlines predict a doubling of passenger traffic by the turn of the century.

Multinational megacorporations move materials and products across national boundaries with impunity. Their employees are also multinational, moving around the world with casual ease. In most places, their passports are mere formalities. World citizenship will soon be a corporate matter rather than a political one.

These huge corporations manipulate entire economies—sometimes on purpose, other times inadvertently. As they exploit, manufacture, and market, they are able to exert increasing influence over governments large and small. Their behavior may be the key to the success or failure of our species.

Bucky was aware of the dangers inherent in the above phenomena. World citizenship could mean the end of cultural diversity. Bucky countered that what people usually mean by "cultural diversity" is actually recognition of quaint artifacts from past ignorance. Graceful women balancing pots of water on their heads may be picturesque, but the water-bearing women are, in fact, beasts of burden. They are soon crippled by damaged vertebrae. The culture-defenders who wish to preserve that way of life rarely include themselves in that unfortunate, but photogenic, group.

Colorful religious customs may be viewed in the same way. Most religions are based on a mordant vision of life on Earth as punishment or at least as a trial. Only the promise of a better afterlife makes today tolerable. Religious leaders have a vested interest in continuing things as they are. Custom is most often based on myth and political expediency. "Morality is what people say other people should do."

Bucky thought that many traditional cultures acted to uphold artificial nation-states whose rulers feared any changes that would raise the people's standard of living to the royal level. Past history shows that any such advance was to the detriment of the ruling class. Pulling the bottom up was never considered because there was never enough wealth to go around.

Design science has made that sorry state of affairs obsolete. It has made nations obsolete. Bucky hoped it would make politics obsolete. He considered the United States to be just that; United-States. We are certainly not one nation, but a collection of nations. With a bit of enlightenment, we could lead the change to what Bucky called "desovreignization"—the change from many govern*ments* to world govern*ance*. Patriots are horrified by this idea. They're still stuck in win-or-lose.

Of course, selfishness could continue to magnify the dark side of technology to bring us all down. The profiteering of industrial societies could subjugate the world, and complete the environmental destruction already under way. Bucky figured about 44% of humanity was still living in poverty. Increasing us-versus-them tension caused by greed and injustice could easily bring uncontrollable anarchy, as the underdogs—armed with powerful weapons for the first time in history—turned to organized terrorism. Think what would happen to air travel if a half-dozen airliners were randomly shot down by the Stinger missiles already in the hands of "extremists"! An angry, clever, 15-year-old could do it.

On the other hand, enlightened multinational corporations—the richest and most powerful social entities now in operation—could be the agents that bring about the new era that Bucky demonstrated was at least possible. For the first time, there are worldwide organizations with talented people and the capability to make and distribute the goods and know-how—including environmental understanding—that can bring a good life to everyone. The artifacts of livingry are being developed by individuals and teams acting as design scientists all over the world. Many of the principles they employ were discovered or proposed by Bucky. The rest will have to come from us, perhaps from you.

The World Game Institute®

Bucky used the term "World Game" in two ways. The first refers to developing the know-how, hardware, and education to make the world work for everyone. (The dedication of this book [p. v] is the World Gamer's creed.) Just about anything that works to that end could be considered "playing World Game." GENI, a Global Dwelling Service, or a conference convened to solve a specific world problem would qualify as examples.

The other meaning refers to an organization Bucky founded in 1972—The World Game Institute®. This organization collects and disseminates accurate, comprehensive, world resource data to be used in World Game Workshops and large-scale planning. This World Game was intended as an antidote to the war games played by Cold War planners.

Bucky intended World Game to be played on a giant Dymaxion Map or a "Geoscope" globe covered with thousands of small lights. (A computer screen for each player would do, but would lack the dramatic impact and resolution of a large-scale display.) Strategies entered on the players' computers would interact, then appear as moving patterns of lights that everyone could see, rather like the graphics on a Goodyear blimp.

Real data (much of it from satellites) would be used in credible simulations of various moves that a country might make. Because such information would be free of political taint, it could be employed confidently without fear of losing face or accusations of corruption. People tend to trust hard computer data more than they trust the machinations of politicians. (Bucky pointed out that people confidently trust their lives to computers every time they travel by airplane.) United Nations delegates might conduct official games that would reveal mutually beneficial moves. Computers would analyze the subtle interactions and "side effects" of individual decisions. Animation would show effects over time. All players, and their constituents, could view the outcome of various proposals.

In addition to showing the results of strategic moves, World Game hardware and software could convincingly present all manner of other data. The spread of a disease could be displayed dramatically in moving lights. Filling of wetlands, distribution of cotton, mining of gravel, and the shipping of rice could be presented visually in a memorable and understandable way. The locations of surplus food, starving populations, and empty ships could be shown together, perhaps suggesting a remedy.

Bucky was confident World Game would show that international coop-eration was so obviously advantageous that war would become unthinkable. Humans could then enter a new phase of their role in Universe.

While the world waits for an electronic Geoscope or Dymaxion Map, the World Game Institute conducts its more modest workshops. Thousands of people have participated over the last ten years. Players have included senators, bankers, generals, small children and college students. About 100 workshops are given each year.

The World Game Institute now has one of the largest world resource data banks in existence. (It may be *the* largest.) There are about 1000 entries for every country. Data include such things as mineral and agricultural resources, literacy levels, human rights records, soil conditions, medical facilities, average incomes, environmental problems, and life expectancies. Much of the data is available as useful software. (For further information on the World Game Institute, see Appendix B.)

Obviously, World Game can be played in various ways on the Internet. At this time, networking is probably the fastest way to convince large numbers of influential people that success for everyone is possible if only we organize to bring it about.

Of all his inventions and discoveries, Bucky considered World Game to be second only to synergetics as a force for making humans a successful species.

Players crowd the huge Dymaxion Map at a World Game Workshop®. Each of the hundred participants represents 1% of the world's population. Each is equipped with appropriate resources and constraints in the form of cards. Players bicker, wheel and deal, and cooperate to make the world work for everyone without resorting to war (which is one of the options). There is a press corps. The complexity level rises quickly. The room gets noisy. Two things soon become obvious: (1) cooperation works, and (2) actually changing the world from coercion and war to peaceful cooperation is not going to be easy. It is a crude—but effective—version of a sophisticated electronic World Game that Bucky envisioned being played officially by United Nations delegates.

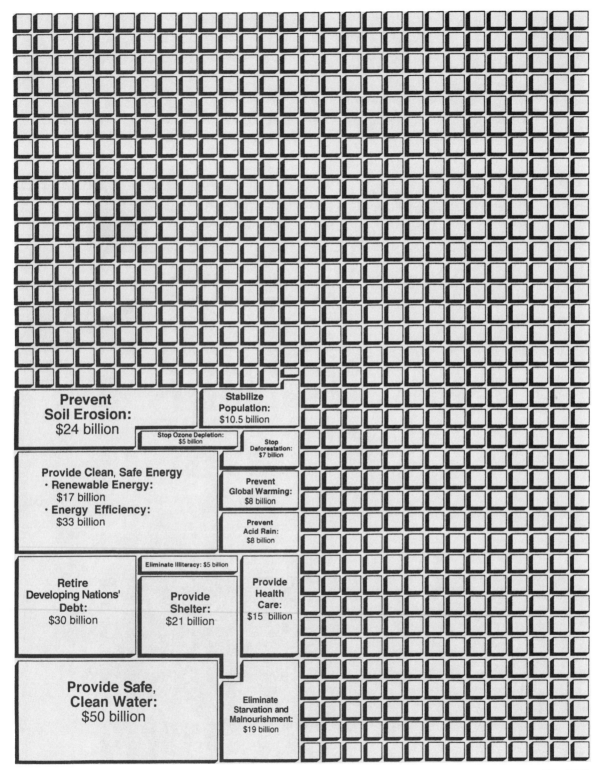

Prevent Soil Erosion: $24 billion

Stabilize Population: $10.5 billion

Stop Ozone Depletion: $5 billion

Stop Deforestation: $7 billion

Provide Clean, Safe Energy
· **Renewable Energy:** $17 billion
· **Energy Efficiency:** $33 billion

Prevent Global Warming: $8 billion

Prevent Acid Rain: $8 billion

Eliminate Illiteracy: $5 billion

Retire Developing Nations' Debt: $30 billion

Provide Shelter: $21 billion

Provide Health Care: $15 billion

Provide Safe, Clean Water: $50 billion

Eliminate Starvation and Malnourishment: $19 billion

Fig. 10-3

The discouraging, infuriating chart, with its appalling statistics, is typical of the macro-views revealed by a study of the data banks of the World Game Institute. Each square represents one-tenth of one percent of the annual world military expenditure of one trillion dollars. The total annual cost of global programs for solving the major human needs and environmental problems facing humanity would be approximately 25% of the annual world military budget. If asked by a child, how would you explain our failure to act on this information?

These notes represent the general direction, scope, and strategy of the chart on the facing page. A more detailed, attributed, explanation is found in *Doing the Right Things*, a paper available from the World Game Institute (see Appendix B).

Prevent and reverse soil erosion: $24 billion per year for ten years, to convert to pasture and woodland, one-tenth of the world's cropland most susceptible to erosion and no longer able to sustain agriculture; and to conserve and regenerate topsoil on remaining lands through sustainable farming techniques. To be accomplished through a combination of government regulation, and incentive programs that remove the most vulnerable lands from crop production, and by farmer education through expanded in-country agricultural extension services.

Stabilize population: $10.5 billion per year for ten years, to make birth control universally available.

Stop ozone depletion: $5 billion per year for twenty years, to phase in substitutes for CFCs and provide incentives for further research and development.

Provide clean, safe energy: $17 billion per year for ten years, to fund research and provide incentives for renewable energy devices, and a graduated ten-year phaseout of subsidies to fossil and nuclear fuels. $33 billion per year for ten years, to increase car fleet fuel mileage to over 50 mpg, and to bring appliance, household, and industrial processes and materials efficiency to state-of-the-art.

Stop and reverse deforestation: $7 billion per year for ten years to reforest 150 million hectares needed to meet ecological, fuelwood, and wood products needs. Planting by local people would cost about $400 per hectare. There would be additional costs for legislation, financial incentives, protection, and enforcement.

Prevent global warming: $8 billion per year for thirty years to reduce carbon dioxide, methane, and CFC release into the atmosphere through a combination of international accords, carbon taxes, and increased energy efficiency.

Prevent acid rain: $8 billion per year for ten years, for tax incentives, regulations, and direct assistance programs that place pollution control devices on coal-burning equipment.

Retire Developing Nations' debt: $30 billion per year for ten years to retire $450 billion or more of current debt discounted to 50% of face value. (Much of the developing world's current debt is already discounted to 10-25% of face value.) Helps countries get out of debt, and helps banks stay solvent.

Eliminate illiteracy: $5 billion per year for ten years— $2 billion for communications satellites; $2 billion for buying and distributing ten million television sets with satellite dishes and photovoltaic power supplies; the rest (90% of total) for culturally appropriate literacy programming and maintenance of the system.

Provide shelter: $21 billion per year for ten years to make materials, tools, and efficient building techniques available to people without adequate housing.

Provide health care: $15 billion per year for primary care through community health workers in areas without access to health care; $2.5 billion per year to supply vitamin A to children who lack it, thereby preventing blindness in 250,000 children a year; providing oral rehydration therapy for children with severe diarrhoea; and immunizing 1 billion children against measles, tuberculosis, diphtheria, whooping cough, polio and tetanus—thereby preventing the death of about 7 million children per year; $40 million per year for adding iodine to table salt, thereby reducing the number of cases of goiter (190 million) and overt cretinism (3 million).

Provide safe, clean water: $50 billion per year for ten years for water and sanitation projects and hardware.

Eliminate starvation and malnourishment: $2 billion per year for ten years for an international grain reserve and emergency famine relief; $10 billion per year for twenty years for farmer education and market incentives for local food production; $7 billion per year for indigenous fertilizer development.

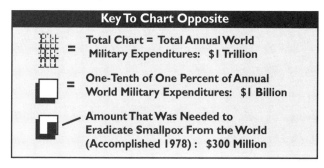

Key To Chart Opposite

= Total Chart = Total Annual World Military Expenditures: $1 Trillion

= One-Tenth of One Percent of Annual World Military Expenditures: $1 Billion

Amount That Was Needed to Eradicate Smallpox From the World (Accomplished 1978): $300 Million

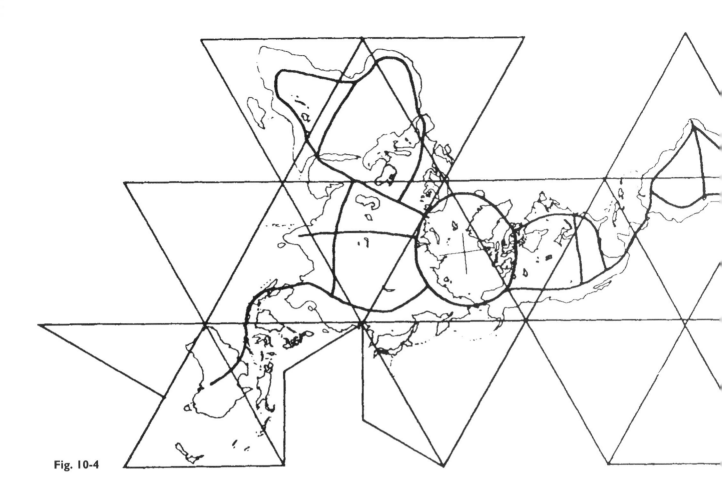

Fig. 10-4

This Dymaxion Map shows the proposed interties of world electrical distribution grids. Smaller systems could join when they become large enough to play. Areas with autonomous systems would not need to join (they wouldn't want to), but would benefit from the overall improvement in standard of living in their part of the world. All electricity users would benefit from more efficient end-use hardware—"Negawatts" (the term coined by Amory Lovins) are the cheapest watts of all. For another Dymaxion Map, see Fig. 4-1.

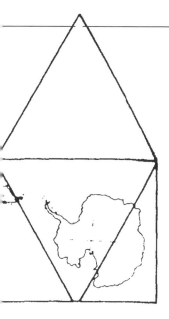

GENI

Bucky considered World Game's highest priority to be connecting the major electrical grids of the world, as he first proposed in 1927. Among the advantages of global interconnection:

- East-west power demand and supply can be matched worldwide to the time of day or night; north-south demand to the seasons (which, as you may recall, are opposite).

- It would be far more efficient—shared power means that generators running full time at their most efficient speed will take care of worldwide needs. Fewer of them would be needed. That means less pollution, too.

- Power companies would not need expensive, little-used extra capacity to level peak demand; if Los Angeles had a hot spell, the additional power needed for air conditioners could be "wheeled" (the official term) from a part of the world where demand was less.

- The cost to consumers should drop as efficiency rises and power companies get more business—a win-win scenario.

- Political strife would be reduced; trade partners rarely fight.

- Population pressures should ease; statistics show that birthrates drop dramatically as rising electricity use brings a higher standard of living.

- Power from renewable sources—often from less developed countries that need the income—can be moved to where it is needed.

- Cooperative effort to build the connections would bring nations together.

Global Energy Network International—GENI—is prominent among organizations around the world that are working to bring this about. Both the high-voltage transmission technology, and computer controls are now available. The major obstacle is the lack of political will to put it in place. It is largely a matter of educating leaders and citizens to understand the advantages. That is the mission of GENI's workers and their colleagues in other countries.

The enormous project is moving forward. Parts of the network are already under construction. GENI research shows that a link across the Bering Strait could be done for 5% of the annual military budgets of the U.S. and Russia, at an annual savings of billions for both countries. East and West Germany have already connected. Israel and its Arab neighbors are working on an intertie, a project that could help bring a stable peace to the area. Virtually all countries are talking about links. The United Nations is involved. The worldwide energy grid is happening.

A Global Dwelling Service

It took Bucky a while to understand why his designs did not revolutionize the building industry: There was no building industry to revolutionize. There still isn't. It's time.

We've had the technology to make Dymaxion Houses for about fifty years. Why can't you buy one? As Bucky found out with his Stockade blocks (see p. 4), the product is only part of an industry. He didn't have much luck dealing with marketing, distribution, servicing, customer relations, codes, zoning, environmental regulations, and all the rest of the infrastructure required to support a business. As we've seen, Bucky was a concept man.

There is also the matter of maintaining quality in a competitive situation. People tend to buy on price alone, giving little thought to the cost of operation over the lifetime of the product. Using clever advertising, the cheapest product with tolerable quality wins most of the market.

What sells best is not necessarily the best. Moreover, there is no incentive for manufacturers to achieve state-of-the-art. Styling and other superficial changes keep customers coming. The huge capital outlay for a big change can be put off as long as possible. (The outlay can be huge indeed: Developing a completely new model of automobile costs several *billion* dollars.) Major improvements come slowly, as the discussion of gestation rates on page 12 shows.

Like any high-performance technology, a Dymaxion House would be *optimized*—a goal that does not cross the minds of most architects, much less the designers of mobile homes. Optimizing results in a different class of product. For example, the automobile and the airplane are about the same age. A century after their inception, automobiles are nowhere near as efficient or reliable as they can be. The finest European luxury cars are conceptually identical to a Model T—essentially the same except in detail.

Aircraft are built to be as efficient as possible. Reliable quality is a necessary goal—you can't get out and walk if something goes wrong. The latest stealth bomber owes little to the Wright brothers.

A Dymaxion House owes little to past architects. It would be more akin to an aircraft than to a car. Except in price.

Aircraft are paid off over many years of service. Autos don't last long enough for that—they are prime examples of planned obsolescence. (Easily degraded conventional houses are examples of *un*planned obsolescence.) The Dymaxion house would be close to the price of an auto—recall that Bucky correctly calculated that a high-tech house should cost about the same per pound as a car, and could thus be paid off as if it were a car. But that would still make it far too expensive for the very people who need it most. Bucky had an easy answer to that dilemma. Lease it—but not as a car is leased. Lease it in the same way that telephones were leased per month, before the breakup of the Bell Telephone System.

System is the key concept here. Alexander Graham Bell wisely concluded that he was not selling telephone equipment; he was selling communications service. He recognized that selling hardware would soon result in low-quality equipment that would degrade the quality of the whole system. Bell made its own phones at the highest possible quality to maximize performance and minimize the need for repairs. The company upgraded its owned equipment as technology advanced. Remember dials, "number please" phones, and the ones with a crank?

The monthly phone bill also reflected each customer's tiny share of the enormously expensive system of wires, poles, switching apparatus, operating personnel, research, and manufacturing—all utterly unaffordable even to millionaires, if it had to be bought outright.

The scheme worked: The relative cost of calls has dropped every year since the company started, despite the company being a monopoly. In all but the poorest countries, telephone service is now available to everyone, at least on an emergency basis. Recent competition may or may not have reduced the cost of the system to the average user. Retail telephone hardware is certainly not as durable these days.

A Global Dwelling Service could take many forms. Complete Dymaxion Houses could be shipped assembled or as kits, with or without an Autonomous Package of some sort. They could be stacked to reduce land use and sprawl. They might be Garden-of-Eden climate-controlling shells that could be erected anywhere in the world to protect whatever was required.

Another scheme would ship molds and drums of molding compound instead of finished houses or kits of parts. Regional factories would then produce and service houses that were perfectly matched to local conditions and needs. Local industry could furnish the appliances and furniture, though the appliances would have to be of good quality and high performance to gain the advantages inherent in the Dymaxion structure.

Service would always be a part of the lease, and could include delivering supplies and removing waste. Appliances and the units themselves would be upgraded, replaced, or recycled as the technology improved. There would be a market for used houses and components.

Autonomous models would totally change the way people think of housing. *House* is architecture. *Housing* is a social matter. Widespread use could make cities obsolete in their present role as warehouses for goods and people. Bucky thought that, "Like a ship, houses will not be sold on a piece of land, any more than a ship is sold on a piece of water." Worldwide standards would be applied to manufactured Dymaxion Houses. International agreements would make codes obsolete, just as autos and television sets do not have to meet the quirks of local codes.

Houses could be moved or replaced with more appropriately sized models if necessary. Seasonal migration would be feasible. Because the houses would be light enough to ship by air, less-developed countries would be able to raise their standard of living without building expensive and destructive road networks. They would enter the new era with air travel as the principal mode of long-distance transport. Birds don't have to learn to run before they can fly.

Bucky saw a simple Dymaxion House as a replacement for the mobile home or prefab house, but there is no reason that deluxe models could not be developed. A worldwide market would demand the production quantities necessary to attract the capital and reap the benefits of mass production. It is an industry that has gestated long enough.

The first Global Dwelling Service consortium will be taking a risk, but they will also have the potential to completely change the fragmented way we build, just as the VW Beetle transformed a business dominated by fat cars.

Initial financing may come from industries crippled by the collapse of the Cold War, finally bringing to pass the "weaponry-to-livingry" dream Bucky tried to bring in with the Wichita House. There was enough money to build Cold War killing hardware; the same money can now be used for more humane purposes. Once they are available, Dymaxion dwellings will be accepted worldwide for the same reason automobiles have been accepted worldwide: They fill a need. A true building industry is ready to be born.

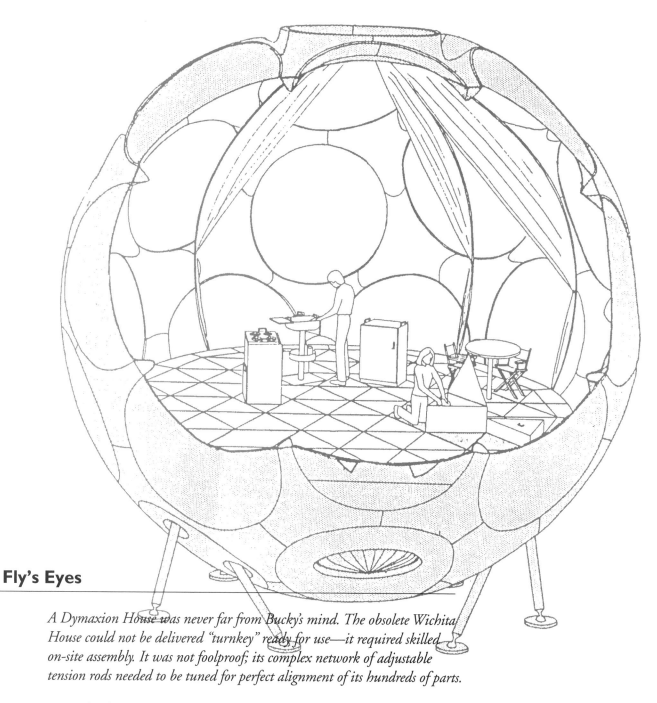

Fly's Eyes

A Dymaxion House was never far from Bucky's mind. The obsolete Wichita House could not be delivered "turnkey" ready for use—it required skilled on-site assembly. It was not foolproof; its complex network of adjustable tension rods needed to be tuned for perfect alignment of its hundreds of parts.

A simpler design made from only a few types of self-positioning components was needed. Bucky thought the Fly's Eye concept had the potential to fulfill the requirements of a Global Dwelling Service. He was actively working on it at the time of his death. Several experimenters continue to develop Fly's Eyes in a variety of sizes. Will they be the first to mass-produce a Dymaxion House?

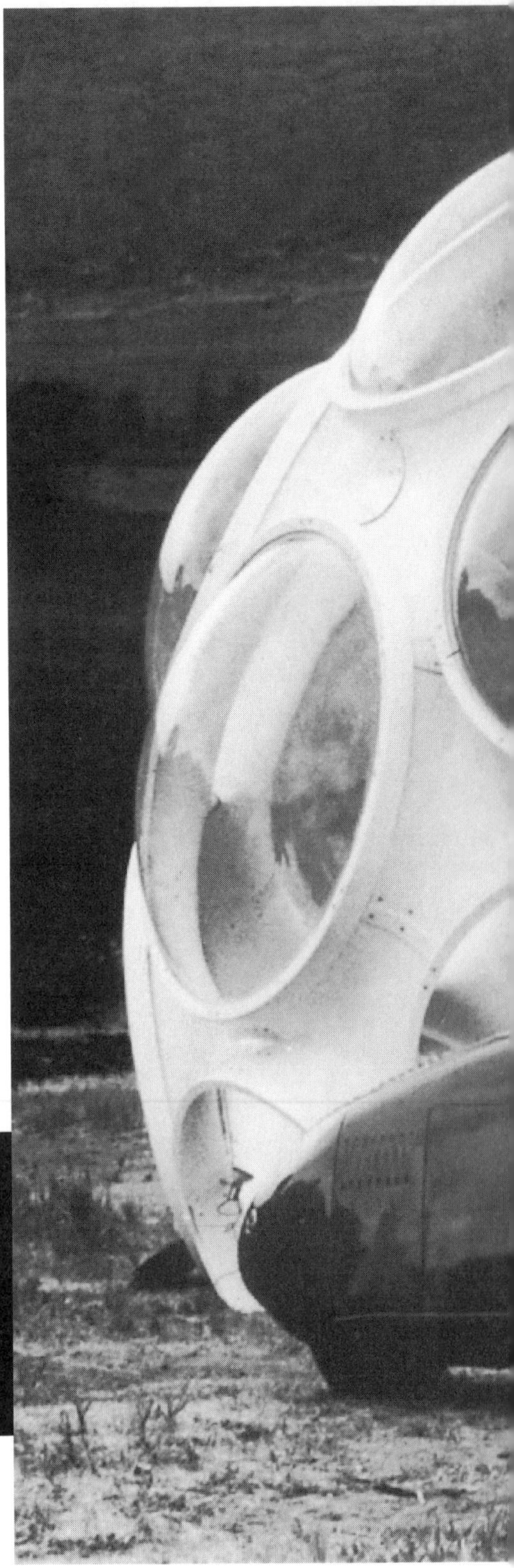

A taste of the future? Bucky and his 1934 Dymaxion car pose with his 26-foot (7.9-meter) Fly's Eye dome during his 85th birthday party at the Windstar Foundation in Snowmass, CO, in 1981.

Fig. 10-5

Fig. 10-6

John Warren poses with the 50-foot (15.24-meter) Fly's Eye he calculated and built to Bucky's specification. The structure uses just three component sizes. Glazing and insulation remain to be worked out, but are not expected to present serious problems. The simple design allows amazingly quick assembly for a 4-story building.

Fig. 10-7

Bucky intended the 50-foot Fly's Eye to
be a Garden-of-Eden dome, but the large
structural shadows shown here would
inhibit the growth of many sun-hungry
varieties of plants. Additional stiffening ribs
(visible at the panel joints) prevent compact
stacking and shipping of parts, a solvable
problem typical of those encountered in
first prototypes. It has since been solved.

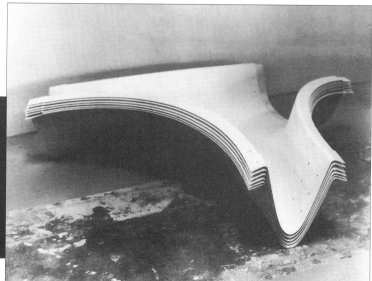

Fly's Eye structural components are
designed to nest tightly without damage,
minimizing transportation and storage
costs. Circular "eye" panels of various
sorts would nest or stack flat, too. At
this writing, the Fly's Eye is undergoing
development by several firms.

Fig. 10-8

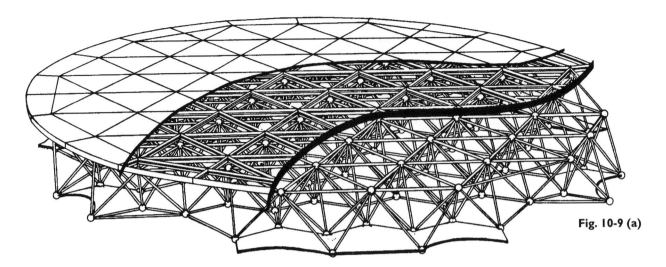

Fig. 10-9 (a)

The floor of this 26-foot (7.9-meter) Fly's Eye is an octet truss requiring no support columns. A complete or partial second deck could be made the same way. The diameter was chosen for its 7-foot (2.1-meter) circular openings—they're large enough to accommodate practical doors.

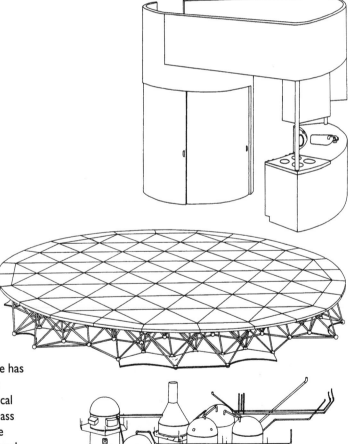

The kitchen and Dymaxion Bathroom module has sleeping or storage space above. Under-deck space is used for storage, tanks, and mechanical utilities. Water bags could provide thermal mass for passive solar heat storage. Using an entire sphere eliminates any need for a foundation, and gives remarkable structural integrity.

(b)

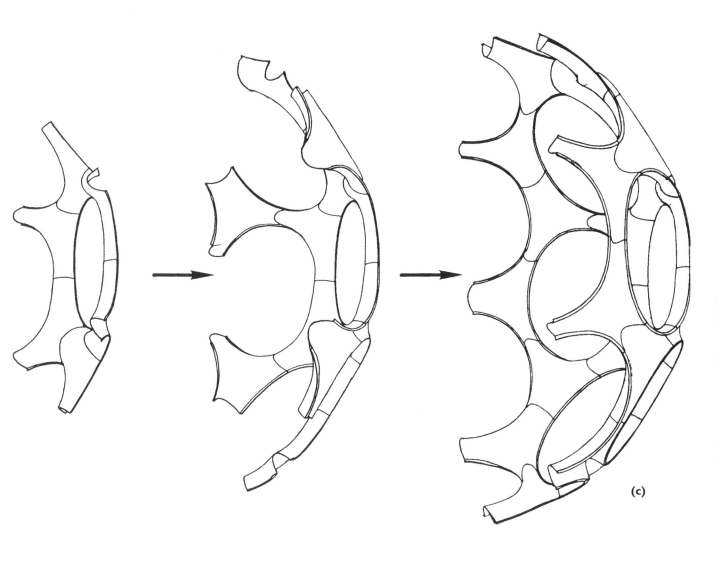

(c)

Only one size of three-branched, hyperbolic "saddle" is used to build up the structure of this 26-foot Fly's Eye, greatly reducing tooling and manufacturing costs. Automated production is assumed. With precision-drilled holes and watertight, "downhill" joints, there is little chance that assembly can go wrong.

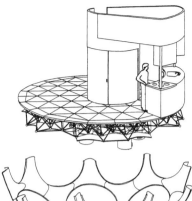

Three sets of adjustable legs serve as the triangulated "foundation." The only earthmoving work would be drilling pier holes for the six concrete pads supporting the feet. On hard ground, the sphere could be held in position by three cable anchors similar to those used to brace utility poles. Earthquake resistance is total except in the unlikely event the ground fractured and spread directly between the legs.

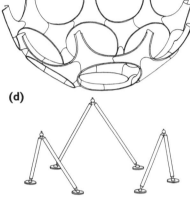

(d)

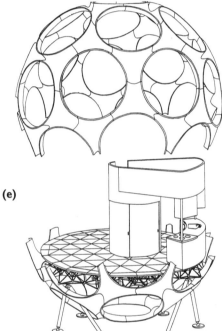

(e)

The Fly's Eye takes shape. On-site assembly would be done from the top down, hoisting the finished upper sections up a temporary mast in typical Bucky fashion. The loadbearing shell and trussed floor permit just about any light-weight interior imaginable.

Bucky envisioned thick privacy fabric partitions, much like those used on the Dymaxion Deployment Units (see Fig. 2-14). A second deck could also be used as a space divider. With the mobile furnishings shown, the floor could be quickly cleared for parties or ballet, for example.

"Eyes" could be filled with a variety of glazing, doors, vents, irises, or solar panels. Individual, circular eye-fillers do not carry structural loads other than those applied directly to them. Snow and wind loads on an eye are transferred to its six surrounding saddle components, which in turn distribute the load throughout the entire structure in a typical geodesic manner.

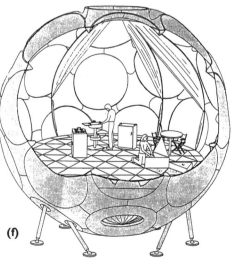

(f)

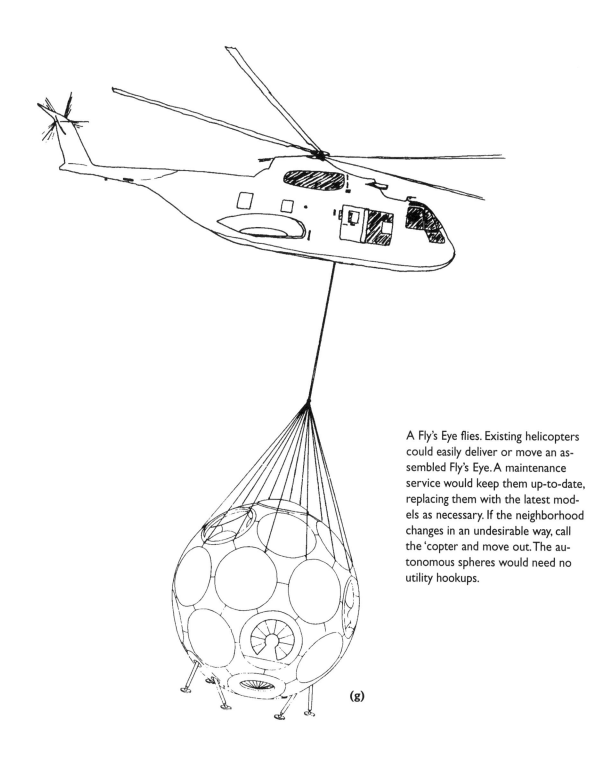

A Fly's Eye flies. Existing helicopters could easily deliver or move an assembled Fly's Eye. A maintenance service would keep them up-to-date, replacing them with the latest models as necessary. If the neighborhood changes in an undesirable way, call the 'copter and move out. The autonomous spheres would need no utility hookups.

(g)

Fig. 10-10

Designer-builder John Kuhtik poses with a model in front of a freshly-minted saddle component of a 33-foot (10-meter) Fly's Eye he is developing. Private individual experiments are often slow and painful, but may bring important breakthroughs as "evolution makes many starts." Plenty of time to think, and no bureaucratic penalty for failed attempts are among the reasons why.

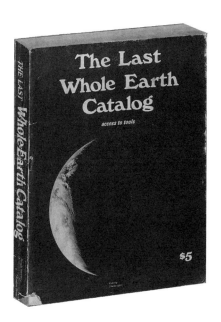

The Whole Earth Catalog

"The insights of Buckminster Fuller are what initiated this catalog," wrote Stewart Brand in his first *Whole Earth Catalog* in 1968. It was a pioneering attempt to gather the information needed for independent thinking and living, a goal dear to Bucky's heart. Stewart Brand insisted on good information, gathered from the experience of readers and subscribers. No subject was forbidden.

A policy of reporting only positive results and recommendations engendered the positive attitude necessary for spirited exploratory effort. A policy of rejecting all advertising, political and religious ranting, sinner-smiting, and proselytizing on any subject made the information credible and trustworthy. Reader feedback corrected errors, kept things honest, and introduced innovation. Those publishing policies are still in force today.

In 28 years of publishing, about 1.2 million copies of the various *Whole Earth Catalogs* have been sold. Reader response indicates that they have been put to good use. A *Whole Earth Catalog* is still published from time to time, and the companion magazine, *Whole Earth Review*, appears regularly as an eclectic quarterly that is often first to publish advanced ideas. There's a Web site. The Whole Earth publications continue to fulfill the task of gathering, and, especially, *winnowing* information that Bucky saw as one of our most important duties as humans.

(Another grain of salt: I am among the many *Whole Earth* editors.)

Syntegrity

All systems are polyhedra. —RBF

The venerable and justly famous cyberneticist, Stafford Beer, has based his latest organization scheme on a single statement by Bucky, who insisted that all systems were polyhedra, whether or not they were conceived or perceived as such. Though corporate tables of organization are often presented as a flat branching arrangement with the boss at the top, real systems are always multi-dimensional. Professor Beer's decades of work with the science of organization have included investigations of geometry as an organizing principle. He uses the icosahedron as a model for organizing projects for much the same reason Bucky used it for structure: efficiency.

Team Syntegrity® regards each of the 30 edges of the hollow icosahedron as a member of a decision-making team with a specific goal (Fig. 10-11a). The 12 vertexes represent major aspects of the project. Each person thus has partial responsibility for two parts of the project, and works directly within two groups of five people. Those groups can connect with other groups on the surface and across the interior of the icosahedron as shown in Fig. 10-11c. The icosahedral pattern tends to be self-organizing and stable. No person or group is more than a few steps from any other. The short communication paths maximize participation and facilitate a role-equalizing process that is much more efficient than the usual boss-and-underlings arrangement.

Of course, a "Syntegration"® (from synergetic integrity) is more complicated than the explanation above. Professor Beer details the mathematical analysis in his book *Beyond Dispute* (1994, Wiley). His company, Team Syntegrity, Inc., conducts "Syntegrations" with people seeking to organize a project and get it done. Reports indicate that the technique shows great promise. In 1995, the team working on Old Man River's City (Chapter 9) found that a Syntegration helped to revitalize and focus their work.

Team Syntegrity continues to refine their methods. New developments include a version that requires less than 30 people—a boon for smaller enterprises. At the opposite end of the scale, Fig. 10-11f shows how the Syntegrity protocols can be enlarged to bring order to enormous undertakings such as those Bucky envisioned for a just global economy. (For more information, see Appendix B.)

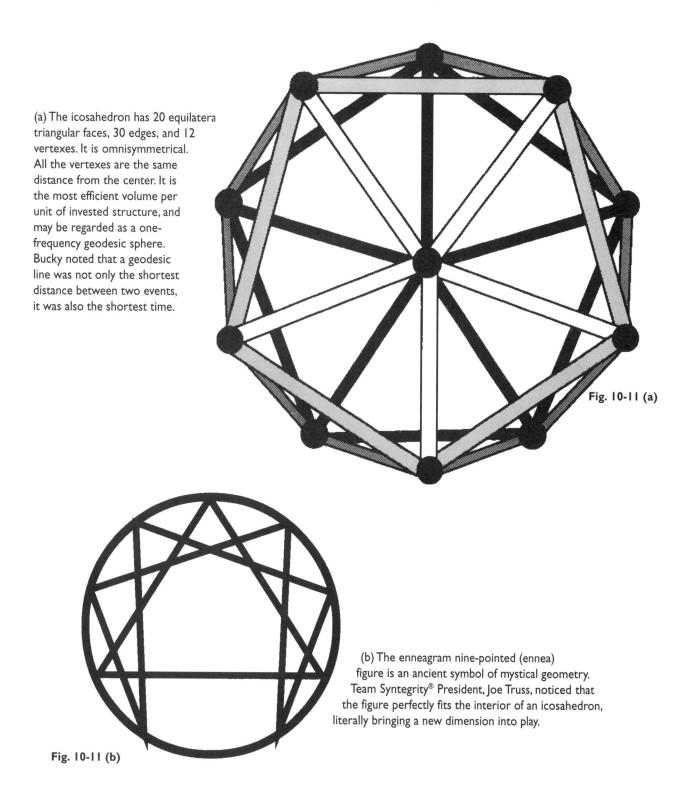

(a) The icosahedron has 20 equilatera triangular faces, 30 edges, and 12 vertexes. It is omnisymmetrical. All the vertexes are the same distance from the center. It is the most efficient volume per unit of invested structure, and may be regarded as a one-frequency geodesic sphere. Bucky noted that a geodesic line was not only the shortest distance between two events, it was also the shortest time.

Fig. 10-11 (a)

Fig. 10-11 (b)

(b) The enneagram nine-pointed (ennea) figure is an ancient symbol of mystical geometry. Team Syntegrity® President, Joe Truss, noticed that the figure perfectly fits the interior of an icosahedron, literally bringing a new dimension into play.

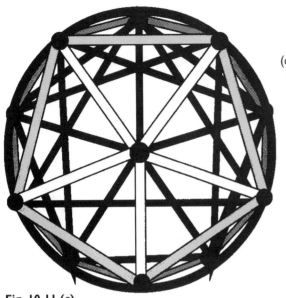

(c) The icosahedron with an enneagram in position, making the traditionally flat ancient figure multidimensional for the first time. The resulting relationships are too complex to describe here; you'll have to read Stafford Beer's *Beyond Dispute* (1994, Wiley) for details.

Fig. 10-11 (c)

(d) A first level of recursion. Each node (vertex) of the icosahedron is a copy of the entire figure.

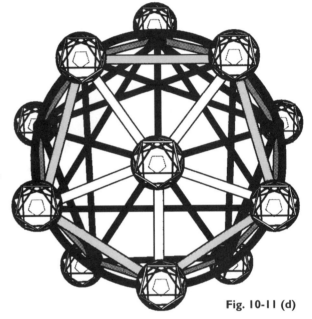

Fig. 10-11 (d)

(e) Cutaway view, with the front struts of the icosahedron (white in Fig. 11-d) removed for clarity. The second recursion into the icosahedron is shown through the dodecahedron contained within. Again, each node contains the entire figure. You'll have to make a model to really understand how they fit together, but at least a model is possible.

Fig. 10-11 (e)

Fig. 10-11 (f)

(f) This full multi-recursive, fractal icosahedron shows three recursions into
the interior, starting with the outer
icosahedron, then the dodecahedron,
with another icosahedron inside it.
Moving out around the nodes (vertexes)
of the outer icosahedron, each node is
itself the entire figure. Recursions into
and out of the original icosahedron can
repeat as needed to handle the organization of enormous projects.

Chapter 11

Jobs and Work

*The trouble with Bucky's lectures is that I go home afterwards all inspired
and ready to work on the important things he talks about, but the next morning
I just go right back to what I was doing the day before.*
     —Often overheard, in almost identical words, while leaving Bucky's lectures.

The work ethic is not lost; work is largely obsolete.—RBF

Security

The usual reason for working at futile, boring jobs is that you have to make
money in order to live. There's rent to pay, food to buy, perhaps a car or a
child that needs your care. Bucky noted, with irony, that 70% of all jobs do
not produce life support. Many are with his metaphorical firm, "Obnoxico,"
a growing megacorporation flooding the world with needless knickknacks.
Working life's hours away at that sort of enterprise soon reduces people to
robots—a heavy price to pay for security. The goal is a good life later, like
heaven. Workers work for financial security, with a health plan, and the
prospect of a pleasant retirement.

Guinea Pig Bucky did not think much of that way of life. It is not what we
were designed and built to do. A very small disturbance—illness or accident—
will severely disrupt a person on the nine-to-five path. Much hard-earned
money is spent on insurance that is not very sure. That cautious and obedient

life strategy brings the illusion of security to many, but dependable security to very few. Yet Nature must have designed us to be a success.

Desirable alternatives to a steady job are hard to see. Most people depend on others for a job. Despite all the talk about leadership in school, we have been taught to obey without complaint. Mistakes—the only way to learn—are punished. The captain of the football team is the kid that most perfectly follows the rules set down by a previous generation.

The smartest people are trained in esoteric specialties that isolate them from understanding wholes, though nature *is* whole, and does not have departments. Academic specialties are a kind of competition; the best performer gets the prize. Competition, rather than adventure, is rewarded. The chance-taker straying over established boundaries rarely wins.

The urge toward financial security leads to psychological fortress-building. Investments, equity, and fear of ageing take precedence. Fortress-builders soon focus their lives on defense. They take up a *conserve*-ative political position, and a mind-set that sees little merit in the imagination that drives evolution. Evolution, however, proceeds anyway, leaving them (insecurely) behind.

There is another kind of security: being too fast and agile to hit. This strategy requires taking chances and thinking for yourself. It can be effective: Bucky said, "All human advances occur in the outlaw area." This sort of security is an individual matter, not dependent on insurance or politics.

There is risk, of course, but there always is, no matter what path you take. You may have to live simply. You may be lonely, as Bucky seemed to be despite his wife's support. Bucky recommended self-discipline, high spirits, and trust in God. His accomplishments are astonishing, especially when you consider that he started his major push at age thirty-two. He insisted that anyone could have done what he did. That may have been excessively modest, but certainly anybody can gather their strength and try.

Nine-to-five jobs may seem safer, but they have an uneasy aspect: As population rises, there are fewer of them. Even in emerging industrial societies with low wage scales, "grunt work" is being displaced by automation. A significant number of the jobs that remain are unnecessary. They will be eliminated in the same way that ATMs have eliminated most bank tellers.

Bucky favored this trend toward the elimination of stultifying jobs. He said, "Automation displaces automatons." He also had scant respect for reformers who recommended a return to an agrarian society. Humans are not built to be either cogs in an industrial process, or beasts of burden on a farm.

The feeling of insecurity that most people feel is based mostly upon threats arising from an unfair distribution of earth's resources. Like air, the resources really belong to all of us. People should get the same pay for the same work no matter where they live. National differences in the value of money are purely artificial, serving only the interests of a tiny, parasitic elite. A skilled machinist should make the same money whether he is in San Diego or Tijuana. Only a line drawn on a map separates the two. The only true security will come when all people can live well without fear, working cooperatively to make the world work for everyone.

On a cool April evening in 1982, after the grand opening of the Pillowdome, four of us drove Bucky back to his quarters in Boston. We'd rented a large, cushy Buick for the trip, because he was still recovering from hip surgery. He was visibly tired—it had been an exhausting, but good, day. As we whizzed along the freeway in silence, he suddenly turned toward me and asked sharply, "*Well*, old man, when are you planning to retire?" Then he cackled like a fiend. The four of us cackled on and off, in waves, for the next ten miles.

Jobs, Work, Duty, and Earning a Living

*You can't run out of money any more than you can run out of inches.
Only humans need money. We don't need it to be a physical success.*—RBF

Bucky knew he astounded his audiences by asserting that they didn't have to earn a living. A few unrealistic souls took that to mean that they didn't have to work. Bucky meant nothing of the sort. There may not be enough jobs, but there is always plenty of work.

Financial journals are unanimous in claiming that the concept of a lifetime "career" is on the way out. People are now hired to work on projects. This is nothing new to innovators—they've always done that. The change from big corporate jobs to private projects is spreading. Jeremy Rifkin, in his 1995 book *The End of Work* (Tarcher/Putnam), discusses the international rise of what he calls "the third sector," people working in areas left unserved by government and corporations. It's a good place to work.

How do you decide what your personal project is to be? Bucky suggested that people *able to do so* should use the following strategy:

First, look for problems that need to be solved. That requires you to be comprehensively alert to everything, not just certain things that interest you. If you are ever bored, it's a sign that an important part of your mind is asleep.

Sensitivity is required; some of the signals are hard to detect. Bucky claimed that "The best ideas seem to be musty, like they came complete from far away." (He suggested that ideas might be projected, as a sort of metaphysical radiation.) Sensitivity is suppressed by seeking to eliminate pain, which is what people really mean when they say "security." You have to be open to everything to be a good receiver. Sometimes you get knocked around a bit. That's part of the game.

Second, learn all there is to know about the problem. Focused learning is a very powerful tool. Attend to what nature is trying to do—opposing nature is futile, inefficient, and is an old-mode way of regarding the world. You may have to experiment. Total commitment is essential.

You may have to work at a second job to finance your investigations, but Bucky said that Universe could be trusted to supply the needs of humans working at making all humans a success. Backup jobs should be selected for their potential as useful experience or practice.

It is well to have multiple skills as reserves in case of delays. Delays are also a good time to do background research to increase your knowledge base.

The third step is proof-of-concept. That's when you transfer from the think-tank to the do-tank. You must demonstrate that you have solved the problem. You actually do it, make it, test it, or whatever is appropriate to get it to the people who need it. Though Bucky rarely had the time to do so, it is a good idea to live with, or in, your work. Make your own prototypes when possible. That way, you'll achieve an intimate understanding of what you have designed.

When (not if) people protest that your idea will require too much money, ask, "What will it cost if we *don't* do this?" (That was one of Bucky's favorite questions.) The answer is the true cost. If there is competition, remember that your goal is inclusive, not exclusive. Also remember that "Obsoleting is different than competitive attack."

Finally, you need to be patient. Project work comes in waves. As we have seen, innovations have their own gestation rate. You are probably ahead of your time. You can't hurry a rose by prying open the bud with a screwdriver. If you have done your work well, your discovery will slowly, inevitably, work its way to where it is most comprehensively effective. Bucky noted,"If you're right, you'll do OK. This is where the courage comes in." He certainly had courage: He did not regard the crashes, fires, and vandalism that plagued his projects as some sort of jinx, but as battle-hardening tests of his philosophy. Sometimes his life must have seemed to resemble that of Job in the Old Testament, but he never slowed.

Can you make a living working like this? Of course! Bucky did. Everyone I work with and write about has either started their own business, is an artist, or is working on a team that is engaged in making things better for everyone. All are teachers, though few are officially. Teaching is an essential part of a designer's work. Bucky considered his artifacts to be pedagogy. Just looking at them teaches you something.

Teaching and learning are what we are here to do. Bucky said that biology balanced entropy. Humans were the most powerful (known) antientropic force of all, because we accumulate and purvey knowledge, adding local order to Universe in the same way that a plant synthesizes air, sunlight, and soil nutrients into botanical life. Bucky's definition of Universe did not permit the discouraging concept of an overall entropic "winding down" into total disorderliness. There is always a building-up of orderliness someplace else in nonsimultaneous Universe. Because anti-entropy is a double negative, Bucky called it, "syntropy". Our purpose and duty as humans is to be syntropic.

The syntropic accumulation of know-how, combined with the 96 natural elements, is real wealth. We can't know less. Einstein showed that matter can neither be created nor destroyed. Therefore, real wealth can only increase. The Chronofile showed Bucky that every time real wealth is used, it increases. Using real wealth synergetically increases it faster still.

Knowing this, realizing this, gives us enormous power. In his later years, Bucky devoted a lot of effort toward convincing a critical mass of people to take advantage of this power before it was too late. He had expected the design science revolution to happen spontaneously and successfully long before. For most of his life as Guinea Pig B, he had been sure we would make it. His hopefulness was one of the things that attracted so many young idealists to his camp. At the time of his death, he was not so hopeful. We're made to solve problems with our minds, but muscle is still in control. Could the successful failure of Guinea Pig B. ultimately fail?

We may be about to find out. Bucky considered *now* to be the Dark Ages compared to what we could accomplish. He worked 50 years ahead to give us some of the tools we would need to "graduate" into being a wholly successful species. He insisted to the end that nature is trying to make us a success, that nature is readying us for an important function. Among all known beings, we have been given access to the principles governing Universe. From our tiny planet, we can tell the chemical composition of stars in a 3.2 billion light-year radius around us! We have been developing for millions, possibly billions, of years. We must be important. We must have a big responsibility. We'd better get to work. Guinea Pig B left us plenty to work with.

Human integrity is the uncompromising
courage of self determining whether or
not to take initiatives, support or
cooperate with others in accord with
"All the truth and nothing but the truth"
as it is conceived by the divine mind
always available in each individual.

Whether humanity is to continue and
comprehensively prosper on Spaceship Earth
depends entirely on the integrity
of the human individuals and not on
the political and economic systems.

The cosmic question has been asked—

ARE HUMANS A WORTHWHILE
TO UNIVERSE INVENTION?

—Buckminster Fuller, St. Valentine's Day
Penang, Malaysia, Feb. 14, 1983
And Chinese New Year

Charles Eames, famous for furniture design and the movie *Powers of Ten*, collaborated with Bucky on this proposal for a 100-foot (30.5 meter) diameter geodesic radio telescope. Its hollow, sealed struts float it in a container of liquid, damping vibrations and allowing precision aiming. The geodesic support structure was designed to expand and contract without distorting the "lens." The project never progressed beyond the model stage.

Fig. 11-1

Appendix A

Selected Bibliography

The following books, tapes, and videos have been chosen for their value as introductions to Bucky's thought. I recommend Robert Snyder's fascinating *World of Buckminster Fuller* video (see below) as the most effective way for a beginner to begin.

Many of the books listed are out of print. The Buckminster Fuller Institute (BFI) can help you find Bucky's writings (see Appendix B), and offers Xeroxed versions of some. The rest will have to come from your local library or used bookstore. BFI also stocks most of the videos and tapes available, many model kits, the Dymaxion Projection Map, and a line of Bucky-related items. Some of the books are pricey, but keep in mind that most of Bucky's ideas are at the forefront of human knowledge and will not easily go out of date.

BFI publishes a comprehensive, reliably annotated bibliography by educator Alex Gerber. It features more than 40 books by and about Bucky. Your local library might like a copy, too.

Selected Books by R. Buckminster Fuller
(in chronological order so you can sense the ideas developing):

4D Timelock, Self-published in 1928. Reprinted in 1970 by The Lama Foundation, Corrales, NM

Bucky's first book presents the larval form of the basic concepts he would elucidate throughout his later work. The emphasis is on housing and thinking for yourself. Metaphysical, cantankerously self-justifying, and occasionally just plain wrong (he thought the stock market would carry us all to prosperity), the original thinking and extreme language established him as a visionary oddball that would bear watching.

Nine Chains to the Moon, J. B. Lippencott, 1938.

At the time it was written, if all Earth's population had formed human chains to the moon by standing feet-on-shoulders, there would have been nine. Most of the book establishes and refines the metaphysical basis for Bucky's later work. Ephemeralization, Dymaxion principles, Einstein's ideas, and Bucky's revisionist history are all here in surprisingly complete form. It's still radical. (A new edition would have to be called *Twenty Chains to the Moon*.)

Education Automation, Southern Illinois University Press, 1962.

This treatise presciently calls for education by what we'd now call multimedia. Bucky outlines the campus planning that would facilitate it, but he was too far ahead of his time to convince entrenched school administrators with no interest in changing anything. His own Southern Illinois University not only rejected his ideas on education, it specified a non-geodesic dome for a new field house. Personal computers had not yet been invented, and there was no Internet, yet he called for the changes in worldwide education that we are witnessing and applauding today.

Operating Manual for Spaceship Earth, Penguin, 1973.

Bucky coined the term, Spaceship Earth, but this metaphor is not at all the mechanistic viewpoint that Bucky's critics claim it to be. (Apparently, they haven't read further than the title.) This vision of Earth stewardship is based on discovering the basic principles used by Universe, then applying them for the betterment of all humankind. Bucky assumes that safe, happy people will treat the planet and one another well.

Synergetics: Explorations in the Geometry of Thinking, Macmillan, 1975
Synergetics 2, Further Explorations in the Geometry of Thinking,
Macmillan, 1979.

In these two weighty books, Bucky fills nearly 1300 pages with his Energetic/
Synergetic geometry (Synergetics), weaving its principles into a logical basis for
everything he advocated and did. E.J. Applewhite collaborated with Bucky to
winnow the enormous mass of information into usable form. The books are
a challenging read, redolent with brilliant insights, interpretations of Universe,
and tantalizing suggestions, all tempered by complicated explanations, metaphor, and baffling sentences. The second book has a paragraph-by-paragraph
index to both. The many drawings help, but you will probably find Amy C.
Edmondson's *A Fuller Explanation* (see below) essential. *Cosmography* can serve
as a respectable introduction and review. An animated CD ROM combining
both books is under construction. It promises to clear up inconsistencies and
illuminate geometry difficult to visualize on a flat page. A publishing date has
not been set; keep an eye on the Internet.

Critical Path, St. Martin's Press, 1981.

This is Bucky's most complete presentation of what we must do (soon) to
make our species the success it can be. The major points of his earlier works
are united into a grand strategy for education and action—truly a recipe for
life. It's the best review of his comprehensive thinking, and a lot easier to
digest than *Synergetics*. The undertone of urgency is contagious. If you're
going to read just one book by Bucky, this is it.

Grunch* of Giants, St. Martin's Press, 1983.

Grunch—*(Gross Universal Cash Heist) is Bucky's term for the manipulation
of world economies by multinational corporations acting for their own short-
term gain at the expense of everything and everybody else. This brief, bitter
satire emphasizes that technology has made poverty and greed obsolete and
unnecessary. If enlightened multinationals acted on everyone's behalf, we could
all live well, and they'd still profit. If they continue their present policies, humanity is probably doomed. This subversive book has not been taken seriously,
possibly because it is not a party-political diatribe. It is an extreme statement,
but in your heart, you know it's basically true.

Inventions—The Patented Works of R. Buckminster Fuller,
St. Martin's Press, 1983.

The book commences with Bucky's last essay, *Guinea Pig B*, which was
written specifically to support the logic underlying this collection of his 28

U.S. patents and their drawings. He personally wrote the patents and their introductions. Be warned that it takes patience to read a patent, even in the simplified form used here. The reward is a clear understanding of what he actually *did* after all the talking was done. A good book for doers.

Cosmography, Buckminster Fuller, Kiyisho Kuromyia adjuvant, Macmillan, 1992.

Published posthumously, these are Bucky's last, highly distilled words on the basis and significance of his discoveries and inventions. It's tough reading for utter beginners, but it's a great introduction to *Synergetics*, and a welcome review for those with some background in his work. Good drawings.

Selected Books About Buckminster Fuller

The Dymaxion World of Buckminster Fuller, Robert W. Marks, Reinhold, 1960.

For thirty-six years, this photo-essay has been where the most people have learned the most about Bucky.

R. Buckminster Fuller-An Autobiographical Monologue/Scenario, Robert Snyder, St. Martin's Press, 1980.

Adult beginners start here. Watch Bucky grow.

Bucky for Beginners, Mary Laycock, Activity Resources Company, 1984.

Kids start here.

The Artifacts of Buckminster Fuller, James Ward, editor, Garland, 1985.

This weighty, expensive, set of four hardbound volumes illustrate most of Bucky's multitude of projects with drawings, blueprints, and photographs. Recent research in Bucky's archives have made some of the accompanying academic commentary obsolete, but these rare books remain a major source of technical information for those interested in a more detailed look at Fullerian hardware.

Synergetics Dictionary, compiled and edited by E. J. Applewhite, Garland, 1986.

Few graphics sully the 22,000 note cards faithfully reproduced in this four-volume set. The ranks of cards are irrefutably tiresome visually, but there is no better way (at present) to encounter Bucky's thoughts on an astonishing array of subjects. Everything is sagaciously arranged and woven together by his friend and *Synergetics* collaborator, E. J. Applewhite. Corrections, comments, and (more commonly and typically) additions, are often added in Bucky's own scribble. I personally find this collection the most fascinating way to explore the many paths that led Bucky to his more radical conclusions.

A Fuller Explanation, Amy C. Edmondson, Birkhauser, 1987.

Working as Bucky's personal engineer for the last three years of his life gave Amy Edmondson an intimate understanding of synergetics and its potential for making humans a success on Earth. Her clear narrative helps readers translate the difficult *Synergetics* books into familiar language, making them accessible to readers unable to deal with Bucky's sometimes obtuse ways. Read alone, the book is the clearest available introduction to energetic-synergetic geometry.

Synergy, Holistic Education and R. Buckminster Fuller: Education for a World in Transformation, Alex Gerber, Gerber Education Resources, 1991.

Bucky's ideas meet holistic thought in this dissertation. A more detailed version paper is due soon. You can get it from Alex Gerber, P.O. Box 2997, Kirkland, WA 98083.

Video and Audio Tapes

Around the Universe in 90 Minutes is a taped chat wherein Bucky works over some of his most famous concepts and discoveries. It's a good place to start if you've not heard him before. BFI sells it.

Buckminster Fuller: The 50 Year Experiment catches three New Dimensions Radio broadcasts of Bucky on one 90 minute tape. BFI will take your order.

Buckminster Fuller: Thinking Out Loud, produced by Kirk Simon and Karen Goodman. This 90 minute video made for PBS is a remarkably detailed look into Bucky's mind. Available from Simon and Goodman Picture Company, 2095 Broadway, New York, NY 10023. Phone: 212/721-0919.

Ecological Design - Inventing the Future, produced and conceived by Brian Danitz and Chris Zelov, is an inspiring 64 minute video introduction to a couple of dozen contemporary designers with a good talk-do ratio. Bucky's spirit pervades the elegantly produced film, and he shows up in it here and there, too. It's won a number of prizes. (BFI has it.)

The *"Everything I Know"* audio tapes lets hard-core Fullerphiles listen to 42 hours of Bucky explaining everything. Some of the tapes are frustrating when he refers to unseen slides and models, but the essence is there, and you can find most of the appropriate illustrations in *Synergetics*. One tape includes his croaked (I'm being charitable) rendition of "Home, Home in a Dome". Available from BFI. (BFI also owns, but does not yet sell, the 42-hour video version.)

World of Buckminster Fuller, is by award-winning documentary film maker Robert Snyder (Bucky's son-in-law). Bucky talks for 84 minutes. That's far less than his notorious verbal avalanches, but Mr. Snyder has craftily distilled it to the essentials. Brief, startling action footage of the Dymaxion car, and a look at some of Bucky's more famous works makes it all convincing. It's an un-usually intimate look at Bucky, and is by far the best way to get acquainted with his ideas. I have found that cool young people really get into it. From BFI.

Appendix B.

Resources

Bucky on the Internet: There are more than a hundred Internet conferences and Web sites as this is written, but addresses change faster than a book's resource list can handle. I suggest using a Web browser to access a search site and then hunting under Bucky, Buckminster Fuller, domes, geodesics, synergy, and synergetics. The number of entries is growing vigorously. A few include much-needed animation of synergetic geometry.

Organizations

Buckminster Fuller Institute, 2040 Alameda Padre Serra, Suite 224, Santa Barbara, CA 93103, Phone: (805) 962-0022; Fax: (805) 962-4440. Books, reprints, Dymaxion maps, toys, models, Dymaxion Artifacts, video and audio tapes, information, and access to the Fuller Archives. An interesting gallery on the premises features Bucky's models and drawings. Members receive the newsletter, *Trimtab*.

Ecological Design Society, P.O. Box 11645, Berkeley, CA 94712; Phone: (510) 869-5015. Fax: (415) 332-5808. email: ecodesign@igc.apc.org. What this group calls "ecological design" is very close to what Bucky called "Comprehensive Anticipatory Design Science." Membership is encouraged.

GENI, P.O. Box 81565, San Diego, CA 92138. Phone: (619) 595-0139. Fax: (619) 595-0403. email: GENI@CERF.NET. These folks are working hard to intertie the world's electric grids, a cause dear to Bucky's heart. Your membership will help. You'll get a newsletter, too.

Monfort Associates, division of Alladin Products, Inc., RFD 2, Box 416, Wiscasset, ME 04578-9610. Geodesic Airolite boats, plans, and kits.

The National Automobile Museum, Lake and Mill Street, Reno, NV. Phone: (702) 333-9300. The Museum has the only remaining Dymaxion car (the second one) partially restored.

Ocean Arks International, One Locust Street, Falmouth, MA 02540. Phone: (508) 540-6801. Information on Living Machines® that organically clean water in artificial wetlands without chemicals. It works. This important work is being recognized at last.

Rocky Mountain Institute, 1739 Snowmass Creek Road, Snowmass, CO 81654-9199. Phone: (970) 927-3851. Fax: (970) 927-4178. email: orders@rmi.org. Fresh-from-the-field information and publications on the Hypercar project and other bold moves toward a resource-efficient, sustainable society.

Synergetics Institute, 5-4 Nakajima-Cho, Naka-ku, Hiroshima 730 Japan. Phone: (082) 241-1609. Fax: (082) 240-8409. Yasushi Kajikawa has developed educational materials and Hypercard animations of icosahedral geometry.

Team Syntegrity, Inc. 34 Palmerston Square, Toronto, Ont. M6G 2S7 Canada. Phone/Fax: (416) 535-0369 Information on Stafford Beer's revolutionary team organizing system. Contact Joe Truss, President.

The World Game Institute, 3215 Race Street, Philadelphia, PA 19104. Phone: (215) 387-0220. Fax: (215) 387-3009. email: xtm0002@duvm.ocs,drexel.edu. Information on World Game Work-shops© and other dynamic programs, Global Recall© software, and access to their enormous world resource data bank.

Periodicals

Dome Magazine, 4401 Zephyr Street, Wheat Ridge, CO 80033-3299. Phone: (303) 934-5656. A regular source of interesting dome news from around the world. Dome producers and builders advertise here.

Whole Earth Catalog/Whole Earth Review magazine, 27 Gate 5 Road, Sausalito, CA 94965. Phone: (415) 332-1716. Fax: (415) 332-3110. For twenty-seven years, these publications have attended important matters that few others seem to notice. No politics or advertising interfere with the eclectic discourse.

Models

BioCrystal, Inc., P.O. Box 7053, Boulder, CO 80302-7053. Phone: (303) 786-9888. Makers of Zometool, the most complex, most capable, and most expensive geometry-modeling kit available anywhere. Particularly useful for Buckyball work. Developed by Steve Baer, pioneer of zonahedra—a non-Fuller geometry that produces domes with useful rectangular openings.

Design Science Toys Ltd., 1362 Rt.. 9, Tivoli, NY 12583. Phone: (800) 227-2316; (914) 756-4221. Fax: (914) 756-4223. A wonderful selection of toys, models and other things geometrical.

Hoberman Designs Inc., 472 Greenwich St., 7th floor, New York, NY 10013-1362. Phone: (212) 941-6329. Fax: (212) 431-7061. Chuck Hoberman offers an astonishing articulated sphere that expands from 9 inches (22.9 cm) to 30 inches (76.2 cm) and back with a flick of the wrist.

BFI (address above) stocks many types of models. Write for their catalog. Several Internet and Web sites give extensive sources for models.

Commercial Dome Designers and Manufacturers

Fuller, Sadao, Zung Architects, 13000 Shaker Blvd., Cleveland OH 44120. Phone: (216) 752-3500. They designed the Montreal Expo dome.

Temcor, P.O. Box 6256, Carson, CA 90749. Phone: (800) 421-2263; (310) 549-4311. Fax: (310) 549-4588. Temcor is the world's largest and most experienced builder of domes based on geodesic mathematics and their own proprietary systems. They've built more than 4000. At this time, they offer only large commercial models.

Starnet International Corp., 200 Hope Street, Longwood, FL. Phone: (407) 830-1199. Fax: (407) 830-1817. Designs and builds commercial geodesic domes and other interesting structures to order. Their technical book, *Spaceframe Basics*, is a boon to designers and contractors.

For dome home manufacturers, see advertising in *DOME* magazine, listed above. There are too many to list here. The Japanese are especially active. There are extensive lists of dome designers and manufacturers on the Internet.

Page numbers in *italics* refer to captions.

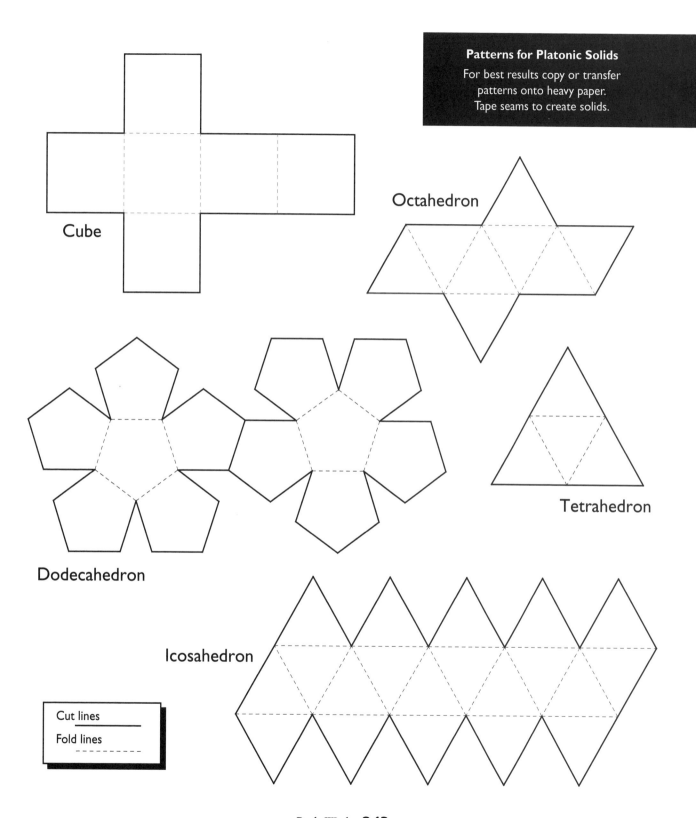

Cube

Patterns for Platonic Solids
For best results copy or transfer patterns onto heavy paper. Tape seams to create solids.

Octahedron

Tetrahedron

Dodecahedron

Icosahedron

Cut lines
Fold lines